Wake Up Now

Razan Abdelkarim Al Fahoum

PASSIONPRENEUR®
PUBLISHING

Wake Up Now

Razan Abdelkarim Al Fahoum

PASSIONPRENEUR®
PUBLISHING

Wake Up Now
Copyright © 2024 Razan Abdelkarim Al Fahoum
First published in 2024

Print: 978-1-76124-196-3
E-book: 978-1-76124-198-7
Hardback: 978-1-76124-197-0

Publishing information
Publishing and design facilitated by
Passionpreneur Publishing
A division of Passionpreneur Organization Pty Ltd
ABN: 48640637529

Melbourne, VIC | Australia
www.passionpreneurpublishing.com

I dedicate this book to each and every person seeking their higher self, and their best life.

Table of Contents

Acknowledgments

I'd like to start by saying that 'acknowledgment' is basically one of the key factors to living a fulfilled life and manifesting your best realities. Acknowledging is an act of gratitude, and gratitude is a key quality in manifestation and self-improvement. Giving thanks, and knowing that you are loved and celebrated, are both reflections of a grateful heart.

I'd like to start by thanking my God. I want to thank God for everything that He has blessed me with, and everything that didn't work out in my favor. He has Complete Knowledge, and I know that His protection is always with me. In this book, I've mentioned my many blessings. Although that was not easy for me as a private person, it was important to do so. As I talk about my blessings, I'm not boasting, but simply helping others understand that our blessings are always more than the challenges in our lives and that God is with each one of His creations at all times. I'm grateful for everything my God has blessed me with, and pray that He blesses everyone who has pure intentions with a fulfilling life.

Thank you, God.

I'd now like to express my gratitude to my lovely mother, Rose Ali Wehbi. Her unwavering support and trust in me are the foundation of my personal growth. Now that I'm a mother myself, I understand that a mother's love is a constant in this volatile world. My mother is always there to offer me guidance and love as I navigate my path through life. She was there during my weak moments and proved to be a tremendous source of strength. Her free-spirited approach has allowed me to be who I am today. Taking her courage and strength of character as inspiration, I explored my own individuality. This freedom eventually led me to delve into the secrets of the universe, our connection with it, and its manifestations, and therefore, writing this book. Thank you, Mother, for shaping me into the person I am today with your unconditional love and open heart.

My late brother, Raed Abdelkarim Al Fahoum, may he be among the blessed ones, was my pillar of strength and his unparalleled love, nurture and support will forever be etched in my heart and memories. His loss was one that shook me. It was something I didn't know how to deal with, but then I remembered that my wonderful brother was always strong in times of adversity. He was a pillar of strength who'd lovingly hold everyone together. He left a legacy of wisdom and integrity, and this legacy is what I take forward with me as a badge of honor. My dear brother, I miss you, and I wholeheartedly thank you for your love and protection.

I now want to acknowledge my husband, my soulmate and the love of my life, Omar Langreo. His presence in my life is a true manifestation of sorts. Omar's love, friendship and understanding have surpassed my expectations of a partner, and I'm proud of the human being that he is. As he and I navigate our journey together with shared dreams, teamwork, and a beautiful son, my heart swells with love. While I was writing this book, I asked his permission to write a small anecdote on our manifestations together. He shrugged, smiled, and said: 'Your book'. These two words reminded me why I love him so much. They were a testament to his trust in me and his true support. Before we met, I had begun envisioning my ideal partner in rather great detail, and soon enough, there he was. He literally walked into my life as the living embodiment of that visualization. There's more on how he made my faith in manifestation even stronger as you read this book. Thank you, Omar, for helping me muster the courage to tell my story, and being a true partner.

Moving forward, I want to express my deepest appreciation to a remarkable woman in my life. She is my mentor, my guide, and now, to my great privilege, my friend—Beryl Comar, a brilliant mind in the realm of emotional intelligence and academia, and a wonderful human being. Beryl set up the first bilingual school in Dubai, and developed an emotionally intelligent work and learning space. She has rightfully earned multiple accolades for her significant contributions to the fields of Neuro-Linguistic Programming and hypnotherapy. Beryl is also the author of the esteemed book *Hypnodontics: A Manual for Dentists and Hypnotists*, and following its success, she went on to establish HypnodonticsWorld™ with an aim of revolutionizing the dynamic between hypnotists and dentists. Beryl's profound and culturally diverse wisdom, and decades of brilliance in the field of psychology, have endowed her with remarkable sensitivity and understanding of emotional intelligence. I take pride in the fact that she's my mentor, and I'm deeply indebted to her invaluable influence on my journey. I wish to express my heartfelt gratitude for her unwavering support and guidance. *Thank you, Beryl, for being my teacher, thank you for the talks as I picked your brains on mental health and wellbeing, and thank you for your friendship.*

Next, I'd like to say that I'm deeply appreciative of the priceless guidance I've received from the highly sought-after Feng Shui Master Yap Boh Chu, whom I hold in high esteem. Through his profound wisdom, I've gained a deeper insight into the relationship between my surroundings and the flow of Qi. He taught me to calculate my energy flow, and reverse negative energy.

I also learned a great deal about the theory of architecture, and making decisions pertaining to land, interior fit-out, color palettes, etc. His expertise has brought about a beautiful harmony in my environment, fostering a sense of balance and positivity. Master Yap Boh Chu's unique approach combines scientific principles and traditional wisdom, making his teachings accessible and relevant to contemporary audiences in the 21st century.

Thank you for being a generous and inspiring teacher.

Now, I want to express my gratitude to Anya Hassan, whose admiration and respect never fail to bring a smile to my face. Thank you, Anya, for entrusting me with the opportunity to advise you.

Lastly, there's one person I would like to thank and although it might be an unconventional approach, I would like to do it anyway. I would like to thank myself. After all, this book shall help my readers strengthen their self-love, and so I would like to start by mirroring my own advice. I'm grateful to myself for all the knowledge I've painstakingly gathered for self-improvement, and never giving up on love, togetherness, positivity, and most importantly, myself.

Testimonial

"Are you looking for a book that will not only inspire you, but also guide you towards living your best life? Well, Razan Abdelkarim Al Fahoum has written a book with you in mind. In this book, Razan shares her personal journey of an Arabic girl learning to make magic in a man's world. She leads you through her self-discovery, how she was able to manifest her dreams into reality so you know that you, too, can achieve anything you set your mind to.

Razan's book is not just a collection of theories and knowledge. It includes practical steps, demonstrates the fears she faced, and her relentless pursuit of authenticity and purpose. Through her unique blend of skills and modalities such as NLP, yoga, Feng Shui, and hypnotherapy, Razan helps people unlock their full potential and live their best lives.

Have you ever wondered how other species communicate and understand each other without words or gestures? One chapter highlights the incredible capabilities of birds, fish, and bees to communicate and work together in perfect harmony - serving as a reminder that there are other ways to convey thoughts and feelings beyond our traditional forms of communication. And while some may dismiss these abilities as "otherworldly," Razan challenges skeptics to open their minds and explore the mysteries of the universe.

So, read and learn about the powerful connection between your mind and the universe through the principles of quantum physics. You will also discover the importance of energy, vibration, and frequency in influencing your emotions as Razan happily dives into the brilliance of your subconscious mind and how it can help you manifest your desires effortlessly."

~ Beryl Comar,

Emotional Intelligence Development Specialist, Author of HypnoDontics, Consulting Hypnotist & Instructor, NLP Platinum Master & Instructor, SleepTalk for Children Trainer, and EFT Trainer

Introduction

Dear reader,

Before I introduce myself, I'd like to say something.

As we commence this beautiful journey together, I want you to know that you'll have a friend in me as we go. In essence, we are all the same; I'm just like you – a human being with hopes, dreams, and the longing to live my best life. In order to do this, I've spent years and years researching the mysteries of the mind, its connection to our universe, and its ability to manifest visions into solid reality.

Thankfully, I have been able to acquire a treasure trove of knowledge, and I have carefully weaved these threads of wisdom into a fabric that makes up this book. It's a gentle nudge to awaken your awareness of the beauty inside you. Your life purpose is waiting to be discovered. Boundless possibilities that lie ahead of you are ready to come your way. I'm here to tell you that you can build a life that aligns with your visions. If I can do it, you can do it.

My name is Razan Abdelkarim Al Fahoum, and I am a living testament that dreams do come true. Visions do materialize. Life does follow your lead – if only you learn how to lead it. Today, I run a global business with more than one hundred and fifty employees, which has gone on to become an industry leader.

I'm also a neurocognitive hypnotherapist, an NLP coach, and a yoga instructor, and it fills me with immense gratitude to say that I have helped many people find their true calling. I live in my dream house with my beautiful family by my side, and I absolutely adore every single second of my existence. The way I am living today is an ode to my belief in God, and my willingness to make something out of my life.

The life I am living today is a life a lot of people told me I couldn't have.

Let me tell you one thing – I've built myself from the ground up. And so, I'm here to tell you that no matter what you're going through, no matter how defeated you may be feeling right now, you're going to make it. You're going to start again if you have to. There have been so many stumbling blocks along my path. Some were tough situations, and some came in the form of people who wanted to break my spirit. Those hurdles were not easy to navigate, and there were times that I wallowed in self-doubt. I just didn't allow them to break me. I'd take a breather, fall apart, cry a little, and then get back out there. This time stronger than before. Like a phoenix that rises from its own ashes.

I grew up in a conservative environment where it was uncommon for women to be ambitious. They were not expected to think beyond certain parameters, and they rarely ever talked about their dreams and visions. Marriage was their primary goal, and I often wondered why they felt their thoughts stopped there. Were they hardwired to believe that marriage was their life purpose? Was it the dreaded 'Cinderella Syndrome'? Cinderella Syndrome was first described by Colette Dowling, and it is the fear of independence in women. It describes when they feel they need to be taken care of. This was a really disabling thought for me.

I mean, I definitely did want to be happily married someday, but I also wanted to do something big with my life. Somehow, these two things couldn't run in parallel from where I came. The idea was too … big? It was this point of contention that fueled me. I promised myself that I was going to live my best life and it was going to be one with unlimited possibilities. I was going to be independent and build an empire for myself. I was going to accomplish all the things people told me I couldn't do. I was going to meet someone amazing and build the right family. That I'd never surrender, that I'd never accept that less is enough no matter what.

Flashback to my early twenties, which were quite the roller-coaster. I'd decided to make it in the trade exhibition business. I knew it was going to be fast-paced; one month of careful planning only to execute in two days. I knew it demanded my focus, handling the business development and operations all by myself. I definitely also knew that it was saturated with other talented people. All of whom were men. None of it mattered to me, because I knew what I brought to the table and I was passionate. I just don't recall signing up for what I experienced next.

It was sometime around mid-June in the early 2010s. I had just started out as an entrepreneur. The heat from the scorching sun had nothing over my anger, as I walked inside the exhibition venue where my small team was hard at work, building a platform that would go on to become an award-winning, prized possession for us. While I walked, I continued decoding the events that unfolded that morning. A tender I'd worked day and night on had been turned down. Not because it wasn't promising, but because it had been submitted by a lady – and what business did *women* have building exhibition platforms? As I approached my site, I was greeted with sawdust, the smell of fresh paint, and the screeching sound of drills. I was also greeted with the realization that I was the only woman there. Something that had not crossed my mind until now. What was even happening? I was working relentlessly to make a name for myself and hoist my company's flag in an industry that I loved. The funny part was, I was doing a great job but somehow, my obstacles felt really jarring. I was anxious and quite confused, to be honest. So many existential questions crossed my mind.

I began realizing that my quest for success and financial stability was overshadowing my family, my emotions, and even my wellbeing. Every time I seemed to find a piece of the puzzle, another aspect of my life would feel neglected or unfulfilled. I wanted to understand what lay beyond the pursuit of financial success. I wanted to uncover a life purpose that would bring me true fulfillment. And so, my real journey began. As I walked this path toward enlightenment, I made some of the most beautiful discoveries relating to the mind, body, and soul. I discovered secrets of the divine source. Connecting with the right teachers was my first step. I'm so fortunate to have learned from masters with profound legacies. There are so many pearls of wisdom that I gained in my decade-long quest to understand the mind and its ability to manifest.

My quest took a magical turn when all the knots in my mind began undoing themselves, one after another. I realized that I am only competing with others if I allow it. That my calling is to be a better version of myself every day. The chaos in my mind about not being able to balance everything in my life also began dissipating. It wasn't about leveling out all areas of my life in perfect symmetry that mattered, it was about finding what truly made me happy and fulfilled, then pursuing that. This simple yet profound truth challenged me to reassess my inner conflicts and the choices I made, guiding me towards a path where my actions aligned with my deepest desires and values. As I delved into my learnings, something miraculous happened. My visions began manifesting. Piece by piece! It isn't like my life didn't have highs and lows after that. However, there was a substantial difference in my approach. The only difference was that I have since trained my mind to be grateful for the ups, and tactfully manage the downs. I no longer panic and unbuckle my seat every time there's a setback. Instead, I face the challenge, and brace myself for my unavoidable success. And so I soar high. Every time.

The heart of my story lies not just in theories but also in the steps taken, fears faced, and relentless pursuit of authenticity and purpose. This book isn't just a recounting of events and the knowledge I've gained; it's a testament that I applied the tools I discovered and sculpted my life into what it is today.

I possess a unique blend of skills that can significantly benefit others, which I express gratitude for each day. I integrate modalities to help those around me unlock their full potential and live their best lives. The NLP techniques I administer assist people in reprogramming their thoughts and behaviors. With yoga, I can help open and balance the energy pathways known as meridians. Through Feng Shui, I help people harmonize their environments to promote balance and positive energy flow. Additionally, my knowledge of hypnotherapy allows me to guide individuals into a state of deep relaxation, where they can access their subconscious minds to address issues at their root and make lasting positive changes.

This book will help you delve deep into the recesses of your soul, confront your innermost fears and desires, and encourage you to design your own destiny.

You are the rescuer of your own life.

With this book, I invite you to sift through the infinite expanse of knowledge, seek enlightenment amidst the chaos, and cultivate a deeper understanding of yourself and the world around you. You may not know it yet, but your life is about to change for the better. I will make sure of it. All I request from you is to read with a mind that wants to be better, and a heart full of love and abundance. I'm here to guide you with all the tools that I possess. When you succeed, I shall also succeed with you. Together, we shall discover the keys to bringing your dream life into reality. All we need is a little bit of trust ... and a lot of faith. You are about to unlock your inner potential and walk toward achieving whatever it is that you want.

And throughout *Wake Up Now*, I'll be walking with you. Shall we?

This is Your Wake-Up Call

Awaken Your Awareness

We don't have to know each other in person to know each other. With this book in your hands, you've taken a step toward me. With what I've written in this book, I've also taken a step toward you. And so, I'd like to start this journey with a quick probe.

Is there something you want to change in yourself? Perhaps a thing you hate about yourself? Is the noise around you too loud? Do you have a big desire to succeed in life but don't know how to start?

You have an inner voice inside you that knows you down to a T. Listen to it.

It can tell you a lot about yourself, if you listen carefully. Naturally, you already know your obstacles, but this voice knows your inner conflicts. It knows what is stopping you from getting whatever it is that you desire. Your inner voice also knows your deepest, most hearty desires. You may not know what you truly want right now. Or, chances are that you know exactly what you want but don't know how to get it. The voice inside of you knows both, and more. For years, I didn't know what I wanted from life, and when it finally started coming to me, I didn't know how to get it. At some point in our lives, we're all faced with existential questions.

Who am I?

Is this even the right journey for me?

How does my mind even work?

How is the universe connected to me?

It's okay to not know the answers. What's *not* okay is covering your ears to the voice inside you that's your guide. Chances are, if you're feeling the way you're feeling right now, this voice inside you is too low, and the world around you too loud. This voice may be low in volume, but it is not far from you in distance. What is this voice? If you're spiritual, it is the soul. If you're a pantheist, it is the universe. If you're empirical, it is the subconscious. If you're emotionally intelligent, it is your higher self. The list can go on, but what if I tell you that all of this is more or less connected? It matters not what label you stamp on yourself. What matters is that you activate this voice, this pure genius inside you. Let it show you the way. It is time to wake up, and take hold of your destiny.

I know it cannot be easy breaking the cycle of hitting the snooze button. Sometimes, the rhythm of our lives seems to echo a common cycle: Wake up, go to work, make money, do what you're expected to do, eat, sleep, and then repeat. We fail to acknowledge that there is something deeper within the essence of our existence; our life's purpose that we are constantly hitting snooze on. That is one of the main reasons we feel unsettled and disconnected.

You may be engrossed in the hustle and bustle, swept away by the currents of daily life—but within you resides a yearning to awaken, to unearth the truth about yourself. Awaken to the beauty of your own existence. For in the end, the journey towards finding life's purpose begins with a single step, a choice to embrace the boundless possibilities that lie ahead, and to keep moving forward with courage and conviction.

We've been blessed with bodies that offer a unique experience for our souls, yet we fail to appreciate the tangible gifts bestowed upon us. If we neglect to nurture our soul's connection to the physical world, we risk wasting the precious gift of life itself. After all, we're all but fleeting beings, temporary travelers in this universe.

Wake Up Now whispers the call to embark on a journey of self-discovery, guiding you through the technical steps necessary to unravel the mysteries of your being, the genius of your mind, and the vastness of the universe. You will tap into many different aspects. You will be introduced to the potent connection between your mind and the universe through the principles of quantum physics. You will meet the broad concept of energy, vibration, and frequency and how they influence emotion. You will encounter the brilliance of your subconscious mind. All this and more to help you understand how powerful your being is, and how effortless manifesting your desires can be.

I've poured my heart, soul, and good thoughts into this book for you to relish and gain from. Not all the things you read in this book shall strike a chord with you, and that's alright. I still urge you to fully absorb the content, and not skim through it. The information is meticulously gathered for your understanding. Once you finish reading, you'll be equipped with the knowledge to successfully manifest the life you deserve. There will be things that might not interest you; when you encounter them, don't pay them heed. Just read them. Knowledge is key. Take what connects with you, bid the rest a fond farewell.

There shall be a hidden click at some point during your reading—it will happen, I know, and it will wake you up. It shall be the spiritual equivalent of waking up physically. You'll wake up, rub your eyes to see it more clearly, and spring into action. Before you reach the end of this chapter, let's set an intention that there shall be an 'aha!' moment in this book. A moment that helps you align with the universe, strengthens your faith, and shows you what you need to do to manifest the life you deserve. A moment that wakes you up.

Awaken Your Awareness

Everything is connected to the mind and the universe. If you find a way to understand it, and design your experiences accordingly, abundance shall come to you. When you know that your mind is connected to the universe, you become fearless.

Yes, we're all connected with one another, and the thing that connects us is the universe that God has created. Just as we're made up of atoms, so is the universe and everything in it. We're all part of the same source of energy. Why then, shall we separate ourselves from each other, and the universe? You and I, we're made of the same matter. Doesn't this concept alone teach us that we're all a beautiful embodiment of love and unity?

When we project our soul out of our body, letting it travel through the bounties of this universe, from realm to realm, it merges with the bigger picture. As we delve deep into this connection, we find that we're all cogs in the same machine.

The universe that God Almighty created is like a colossal corporation, with everything inside it playing a specific role—from inanimate marvels like mountains to living, breathing beings. Every human has a role of its own, and that means we all have a purpose in this world. We're like machines with emotional intelligence, and like all machines, we serve a specific purpose.

The fascinating correlation of our bodies, minds, thoughts, and the universe in its entirety may surprise you at first, but as you get used to the idea, it will feel like second nature, an innate understanding. When we contemplate the vastness of the cosmos, we begin to see that everything is closely connected, from the tiniest particles to the grandest celestial bodies. This extends to our own beings—our bodies and minds aren't isolated entities, but rather integral parts of this larger cosmic web. Our thoughts and emotions resonate with the rhythms of the universe, reflecting the ebb and flow of its energies. By recognizing and understanding these connections, we can cultivate a deeper sense of harmony within ourselves and the world around us.

Going forward we'll discover in detail how our bodies, minds, and thoughts shape our reality. For now, here's a quick tour of what we'll be deep diving into in later chapters.

Body

The spiritual connection our bodies have with the universe is profound, transcending physical boundaries. Our bodies are like microcosms of the universe, reflecting its rhythms and energies. Just as everything in the universe is connected, the human body works in the same way. Every aspect of our physical being is linked to the larger realm. This connection goes beyond the purely physical; it extends to our spiritual essence, our consciousness, and our sense of being part of something greater than ourselves. When we tune into this spiritual connection, we open ourselves to a deeper understanding of our place in the universe and the profound interplay between the physical and the spiritual.

Mind

The mind is intricately connected to the universe through the principles of quantum physics and consciousness. Quantum physics suggests that at the most fundamental level, everything in the universe is connected, even our thoughts and consciousness. Our thoughts and intentions are like signals that interact with this network of energy, influencing the way events unfold in our lives. This concept implies that our minds have the potential to shape our reality by influencing the quantum field around us.

Thoughts

Our thoughts are also intertwined with the universe, forming a bridge between us and the cosmic whole. Thoughts aren't just fleeting mental phenomena, but powerful forces shaping our reality. Our thoughts and emotions attract the experiences we have in our lives. By cultivating positive, harmonious thoughts, individuals can align themselves with the higher vibrations of the universe, thereby attracting more positive experiences and contributing to the overall balance and harmony of cosmic energy.

Sometimes, we're unaware of the profound impact that our mindset can have on our lives. We go through life as if we're stuck in the same cycle and have no control. Fact is, we have control over every aspect of our lives—yet that happens only when we become aware. We may not realize that our thoughts shape our reality, influencing every action and ultimately determining our outcomes.

Another reason why we may feel stuck is a lack of understanding of our true selves and desires. Without a clear sense of identity and purpose, it can be challenging to envision a path forward or know what we truly want. This lack of clarity can lead to feelings of frustration and confusion, further reinforcing the belief that our desires are unattainable. Skepticism also plays a role in furthering this mindset of limitation. Many people adhere to the belief that if something can't be seen, heard, or touched, it mustn't be real. This skeptical attitude can prevent individuals from exploring new ideas or possibilities that fall outside the realm of their current understanding. By closing themselves off to the unknown, they limit their ability to expand their horizons.

Overcoming the mindset of limitation requires a shift in perspective and a willingness to explore new possibilities. By becoming more aware of the power of our thoughts, beliefs, and intentions, we can begin to break free from the constraints holding us back. Embracing our true selves and opening our minds to the unseen can lead to a greater sense of purpose and fulfillment, allowing us to manifest the life we truly desire.

Let's Start Again

Isn't it an eye-opener when you think about how we're all pro-grammed from the moment we're born? I mean, think about it—right from our names to our religion and even our behavior, everything seems to be set in stone. It's like we're handed this script, and we're expected to play our part without questioning it.

But what if we could alter this programming? What if we explore our power to rewire the programs in our minds that aren't aligning with our highest self?

Our thoughts are the light that guides us. When we enlighten our minds with valuable knowledge, it's like turning on that light-bulb—the one that's been waiting for something to fuel it. That fuel is our newly found positive mindset. It illuminates every-thing around us, allowing us to see things more clearly. And when we open our minds to the idea that we're all connected, it's like turning that lightbulb into fireworks reaching far and wide, con-necting us to everyone and everything in the universe. This light silences all the negative noises in the background. At the risk of sounding a little philosophical, I'd say we all know that light trav-els faster than sound. It's one of those basic principles that really makes you stop and think. If our thoughts are like light, maybe that's why they have such a powerful impact on our reality.

When we start to understand how vibrations work and how everything is connected in this universe, we tap into a hidden power within us. Vibrations have this incredible ability to trans-form us from the inside out, shaping our thoughts and emo-tions in ways we never thought possible. Therefore, it's time we started thinking of our thoughts as more than just fleeting ideas. They are, after all, the key to unlocking our true potential and breaking free from the programming that's held us back for so long. After all, if we open our minds to the possibilities that exist in this universe, who knows what we might discover? It's time to let our thoughts be the light that guides us toward a brighter future. One that's aligned with the universe. Let's start again. Let's start afresh.

The Theory that Blows Your Mind

Start to See the Big Picture

The Deeper Awareness

Birds of a feather flock together. Fish swim in beautiful align-ment. All the bees in a hive protect their queen.

How?

Have you ever wondered what their form of communication is? When we look at how these species understand each other, we open ourselves to phenomena that are nothing short of mir-acles for us humans. This must mean that words and gestures can't be the only ways to convey our thoughts and feelings. There are other ways. No, we're not talking about otherworldly ways (although I do feel that we shall leave a little room for enchantments in our lives, but that's beside the point here). This chapter is strictly for the skeptics, I can assure you—the ones among us who want everything backed up by logic and science. We'll unravel the mysteries of transcripts native to the universe. I sincerely hope that in doing so, I shall convince my reader that by understanding the greatness of science, we come to love the greatness of God.

They say there are 7000 languages in which to express our thoughts. There are also artforms like sculptures, paintings, poems, dance, and architecture that can express our emotions. Modern innovation has offered us social media of many kinds to express our identities. And yet, we remain in the dark when we consider expressing our innermost desires to God. What form of communication shall we use? Our minds, of course!

God has bestowed us with a fascinating gift—the mind. It's a complex thing, described in many ways, but its true nature remains a mystery. Understanding ourselves and our place in the world is crucial. What makes us special? How do we con-nect with the universe? What's the relationship between the universe, our minds, and our bodies? Something profound con-nects the universe with humanity, a mystery I've contemplated for years. To unravel this conundrum, I've sought evidence and discovered truths that have changed my life. Though I'm not a scientist, I write about science because curiosity has driven me to explore these questions deeply. Along the way, I've had many 'aha' moments that have transformed my life, and I hope to use these insights to help you transform yours.

The beautiful thing about the mind is that although many disagree on what it is, plenty agree on how it works and helps attract our best lives. When you know how your mind is connected to the universe, and how it works, you become fearless. How is your mind connected, you may ask?

Quantum Physics

Everything is energy.
The mind is connected to the universe through the principles of quantum physics and consciousness. Quantum physics suggests that at the most fundamental level, everything in the universe, including our thoughts and consciousness, is in connection. Our thoughts and intentions are like signals that interact with this web of energy, influencing the way events unfold in our lives. This concept implies that our minds have the potential to shape our reality by influencing the quantum field around us.

By understanding and harnessing this connection, we can learn to use our minds more intentionally to manifest positive outcomes and align ourselves with the flow of the universe.

In this chapter, we'll explore the realms of quantum physics, and how we can use this knowledge to manifest our desired reality. This is not mumbo-jumbo, and definitely not wishful thinking. This is, in fact, the key to unlocking a portal that will give you the life you want. You deserve it.

Quantum Physics: Finally, a Branch of Science That Lets Us DREAM!

The world we live in is evidence-based ... isn't it? There are unavoidable speculations in different walks of life, so we create documents to validate many of our conditions and situations. Businesses have contracts. Families have wills. Even society in general has ways of weeding out doubts in the form of censuses, research papers, and even encyclopedias! Therefore, it's only natural that all claims are backed by ideas that can be quantified and documented. And so, here we are with quantum physics. You might have laughed (or sighed) at the mention of quantum physics. After all, few branches of science have been subject to the same level of doubt and skepticism as this one.

Is it because this revolutionary branch of science is now challenging a lot of theories that have been long-established and taught in schools for years now, contributing to our self-limiting beliefs? Whereas quantum physics lets you dream ... lets you manifest (Mohrhoff 2016, p.24). Think about it.

Now, before we do a deep dive, let's look at some of the misconceptions about quantum physics and its relation to manifestation. Indeed, this is just the beginning, and these two need to be studied further in correlation to offer evidential data. But hey, isn't that the case with literally all branches of science? Let's admit it—Newton and his apple revolutionized the laws of physics until everyone asked: But what about Mercury, with an amount of rotation that can't be accounted for by the gravitational forces exerted by other planets? Then Einstein came along and said, 'Nope, that's not really how gravity works. Time is relative to the speed of light and mass. It ain't constant'. (Of course, I'm paraphrasing here, just to be clear!) What we take away from this is that light plays an important role in the development of relativity and quantum mechanics. Further to this, Maxwell demonstrated that electric and magnetic fields travel through space as waves moving at the speed of light. He suggested that light is a wave of the same substance responsible for electric and magnetic effects. Hold that thought, we're going to get to it in the next section of this chapter as we look into a theory that will blow your mind!

Why can't we give quantum physics the same chance we gave to other branches of science that are literally proving themselves wrong? Pioneering scientists such as Max Planck, Albert Einstein, Niels Bohr, and many more made groundbreaking discoveries that challenged classical Newtonian physics and gave rise to the field of quantum mechanics. These discoveries revealed the inherently probabilistic nature of quantum systems, where particles exist in multiple states simultaneously until they're observed; at that point, the act of measurement collapses their wave function into a single state.

Quantum physics delves into the behavior of particles at the subatomic level. It's like understanding something from its very existence, then building it from the ground up. In this process, it's up to us to make sure that this attempt is aligned in the most beautiful, positive stream of consciousness. Quantum physics basically goes into a deep study of matter and energy at their most fundamental level, aiming to unravel the properties of nature's building blocks. Like all quantifiable science experiments, quantum experiments often focus on tiny particles like electrons and photons. However, quantum phenomena influence everything around us, even though they might not be readily apparent in larger objects such as the atmosphere. For the naysayers, quantum phenomena seem strange or otherworldly—but quantum science fills gaps in our understanding of physics, offering insights that enhance our comprehension of everyday life.

Over two thousand years ago, Hermes Trismegistus said, 'That which is above is like to that which is below, and that which is below is like to that which is above' (Craiker 2022).

Today, Dr Joe Dispenza, scientist and bestselling author, suggests that there's an infinite field of possibility.

Both, in their own ways, thousands of years apart, are basically saying that the world reflects back the consciousness that's being projected onto it.

The connection between quantum physics and spirituality is really interesting. It all comes down to energy and vibration. Observations in quantum systems mirror spiritual concepts, including unity and oneness. Some even say that quantum theory's indeterminacy leaves room for the influence of consciousness on the physical world. This makes way for the concept that the mind shapes our reality. The intersection of quantum physics and spirituality is an inspiring one which paves a path to many positive possibilities.

Everything in life is vibration

– ALBERT EINSTEIN

Quantum physics opens up possibilities, challenging our self-limiting beliefs. In today's world, many people find themselves trapped in a mindset that tells them they can't achieve what they truly desire. Society often reinforces this negative pattern of thinking, inundating us with messages that focus on limitations rather than possibilities. Earlier, we discussed our tendency to be doubtful about different facets in our lives. This sometimes reflects in our self-image. We're also conditioned to doubt our capabilities, which can lead to a lack of confidence and a sense of helplessness. This prevailing mindset can create barriers to personal growth and success, preventing individuals from reaching their full potential.

Reality is Not Only Physical: The Double-Slit Experiment
There's a theory within quantum physics that I'm positive will blow your mind! It's a little mechanical and detailed, so I request you to focus keenly as you read about it. You don't have to be a physicist to understand it, I promise. This theory is called the Double-Slit Experiment, which was designed by a British polymath some two hundred years ago. (Thank you, I. Thomas Young.) This is one experiment that simply makes me gasp at the magnificence of the universe.

The slit measurement theory explores how particles, such as electrons or photons, behave. In this experiment, particles are shot at a barrier with two small openings, and a screen behind the barrier records where the particles land. Normally, if you were to shoot particles through two slits, you'd expect them to create two separate bands on the screen, showing which slit each particle went through. However, in this experiment, even when particles are shot one at a time, they create a pattern on the screen that looks like waves overlapping, *not* like particles going through two slits. This is called wave–particle duality.

Now, here's where it gets even more interesting. When scientists try to figure out which slit a particle goes through by measuring it, the interference pattern disappears. The particles act like individual particles again, creating two bands on the screen. This suggests that the act of measuring or observing the particles somehow changes their behavior. It's a puzzling idea that challenges our understanding of how the world works at a very small scale. That there's a cause, and its effect. This brings us back to the idea that everything in this universe is connected at the subatomic level—if we can only improve our 'cause', its effect will improve in parallel. This applies to our thoughts as well! Your perspective and outlook will inevitably parallel the effect it brings forth.

Remember I requested you to hold onto a certain thought—the notion that light is an electromagnetic wave, as James Clerk Maxwell published in a study (1865), and that the speed of light is constant no matter who measures it, as explained by Einstein (1905). Light plays a crucial role in the development of quantum physics.

Let's do something.

Observe your surroundings.

There are likely various objects around you.

What you perceive as objects aren't truly physical entities.

What are they?

You're witnessing light reflecting off these items and entering your eyes, which your brain interprets as objects or masses. All the information you observe in the room is carried by quantum particles known as photons, which make up the light. This information travels at the speed of light. Without this light, you'd be unable to see or gather information. Hence, light plays a crucial role as the fundamental medium for exchanging energy and information across different parts of the universe, including your surrounding environment.

Quantum world theory suggests that our thoughts and intentions can influence the physical world, leading to manifestations through the power of the mind. This idea is rooted in the concept that we're all made up of energy. When we think about the universe in terms of energy, it opens up a new perspective on how connected we truly are. This extends beyond our individual selves and encompasses the entire universe, emphasizing the importance of understanding our place within it.

Considering ourselves as energetic beings opens up a new perspective on our existence—the idea that we're all connected. This connection even extends to our emotions. For instance, the energy of love. Love is often thought of as a powerful force that can transcend boundaries and bond people profoundly. From a quantum perspective, this energy of love can be seen as a fundamental aspect of our existence, shaping our relationships and influencing the world around us in ways that extend beyond our immediate understanding. This is why love is the answer. Always.

As we conclude this chapter, I'd like to say that my perspectives are based on my basic understanding of the quantum world. I urge you to use the information I've gathered for you to your benefit, then form your own perspectives. Find that connection. This shall awaken you to unlimited possibilities. This book is a framework of tools and knowledge that will help you figure out what methods work best for you, so that you can meet and greet your higher self, every day, for the rest of your life.

Energy Has It All

Symphony of Vibrations

The Beauty in Small Things

I want you to close your eyes and liken the universe to a giant symphony.

Now replace the instruments and notes in it with energy, frequency, and vibration.

Hold that thought for this chapter.

The law of vibration tells us that everything in the universe, whether we can see it or not, is made up of pure energy or light, all buzzing and resonating in their individualistic ways. Even the words we speak carry energy. After all, it's not just about what we say, but the energy we infuse into our words that really gives them meaning. Everything is energy, and varying frequencies of energy affect matter differently. Every particle in the universe, from the tiniest atom to the largest star, moves to its own rhythm and pattern. These particles interact in complex ways, driven by their inherent vibrations and energies.

Energy: Vibration and Frequency

As much as many of us want to imagine fairy dust–sprinkled musical instruments, and conveniently evade logic, there will always be the ones among us who only want logic. And so, logic I give them. As we discovered in the previous chapter, particles such as electrons exhibit dual wave–particle characteristics at the subatomic level (Britannica 2024). This means they can behave as both particles *and* waves!

When tiny particles act like waves and meet obstacles, their waves can mix, creating weird effects like quantum tunneling, where they can pass through things they shouldn't be able to. Also, the size of the wavelengths, and how much energy they carry, really matters in how they act inside atoms and molecules. This affects how chemicals bond, how electrons move around, and even how materials behave. So, when we look at the tiniest bits of the world, the dance between energy, frequency, and matter is super-important in figuring out how everything works.

And it's not just out there in the cosmos; it's in us, too. Our bodies are like a grand composition of cells, each made up of molecules, and those molecules are made of atoms. So, in a way, we're all dancing to the cosmic melody of energy, frequency, and vibration.

Matter: The Human Body
When examining the human body, its structural components become apparent. The outer layer is composed of skin cells, while the muscles, bones, and nerves are composed of muscle cells, bone cells, and nerve cells, respectively. This cellular composition underscores the fundamental building block of the body: the cell. Cells, in turn, are intricate structures made up of proteins—complex molecules that form the basis of cellular function—as well as water and other materials, all of which are composed of molecules.

At the core of each cell lies DNA and RNA, which are pivotal in orchestrating cellular activities. Delving deeper into the molecular level, these essential biomolecules are constructed from atoms, the fundamental units of matter. For instance, water is a compound of oxygen and hydrogen atoms, while proteins consist of carbon, hydrogen, oxygen, and other elements. Thus, the molecules constituting the body's cells are ultimately derived from atoms, these elemental building blocks.

So, did you see how the smallest atoms make up the entire universe together? Start linking things together and see beyond your limitations (Siegel 2023).

Going Round the Magnetic Field

I'm sure you already know what a magnetic field is, but just in case you've forgotten that elementary school lesson, I'll jog your memory. As children, we probably imagined the U-shaped magnet our physics teachers held aloft as a powerful object surrounded by a unique forcefield (also known as, yes, a magnetic field). We were taught that this magnetic field helps us understand how the magnet's power spreads out around it. That's it. Really. If you understood this concept in school, you got a good grade. Now that we're adults, this knowledge equips us to ponder the marvels of the magnetic field in terms of energy and vibrations, making our lives even better.

Resonate with Your Magnetic Field

In the quantum world, the magnetic field is closely tied to how tiny particles, like electrons, spin and move. These particles act like they have a tiny magnet inside them, which we call their 'spin'. When it's near a magnetic field, this tiny magnet can line up with the field or wobble around. How much they line up or wobble depends on how strong the magnetic field is and the properties of the particle, like its size and charge. This interaction between the particle's spin and the magnetic field affects the energy levels of the particle (Tavel 1999). It's as if the particle can have different energy levels, depending on how it's spinning and how strong the magnetic field is.

Our thoughts and emotions act as a magnetic field, drawing complementary energies and experiences into our lives. The energies we emit resonate with the vibrational frequencies of the universe, thereby shaping the fabric of our reality. Much like a magnet's polarized field, our mental and emotional states exert a subtle yet strong influence, aligning our lives with the resonance of our innermost thoughts and feelings. We then experience heightened awareness of the relationship between the self and the broader cosmos, which in turn invites us to contemplate the potential implications of our internal landscapes on the external manifestations of our existence.

Find Your Frequency

'If you want to find the secret of the universe, think in terms of energy, frequency and vibration.' This quote has been widely attributed to Nicola Tesla, as it conveys similar ideas to those expressed by him during his lifetime. One such source is the book *Tesla: Man Out of Time* by Margaret Cheney, which provides valuable insights into Tesla's life, ideas, and philosophies.

Did you know that frequencies can impact mood, emotions, and even physical wellbeing? They're measured in Hertz (Hz), the SI unit for frequency which is equal to one cycle per second. Humans are only capable of hearing frequencies of 20 Hz and above. And yet, exposure to inaudibly low frequencies like 19 Hz might still evoke feelings of fear. Can you imagine how powerful that is?

Our bodies naturally resonate at around 7.5 Hz, which is close to the Earth's natural frequency. Conversely, the universe vibrates at 432 Hz, a frequency well-known for its calming and healing effects. Did you really think that being connected with nature is only something people romanticize in literature? I thought so, until I realized how frequencies work, and I'm still learning. There's a reason wise people tell you to immerse yourself in nature. We're connected in ways that might astound you! Walking on the grass bare feet, letting the waves caress you, feeling the rain on your skin ... all these things aren't just for songs. They literally get you attuned with the universe.

Speaking of songs, have you ever wondered how music can impact your mood? Music is a strong manifestation tool. When you're listening to certain tunes, and even lyrics, you can manifest the connotations they bring with them into your life. This is why it's so important not to listen to grim music that lowers your frequency.

During my research in the early years, I was blown away by how the frequencies varied. What astounded me most was that the peace frequency, at 600 Hz, was higher than love, at 500 Hz. Acceptance, which emits 350 Hz, is higher than the emotion of pride at 175 Hz. Enlightenment, which I like to believe is your super-consciousness, is at a whopping 700 Hz! Understanding these frequencies can help us tune into their vibrations, allowing us to adjust and analyze our own frequencies with greater awareness. The chart can become your breakthrough in regulating emotions and becoming attuned to the frequencies aligned with your manifestations.

THE HAWKINS SCALE

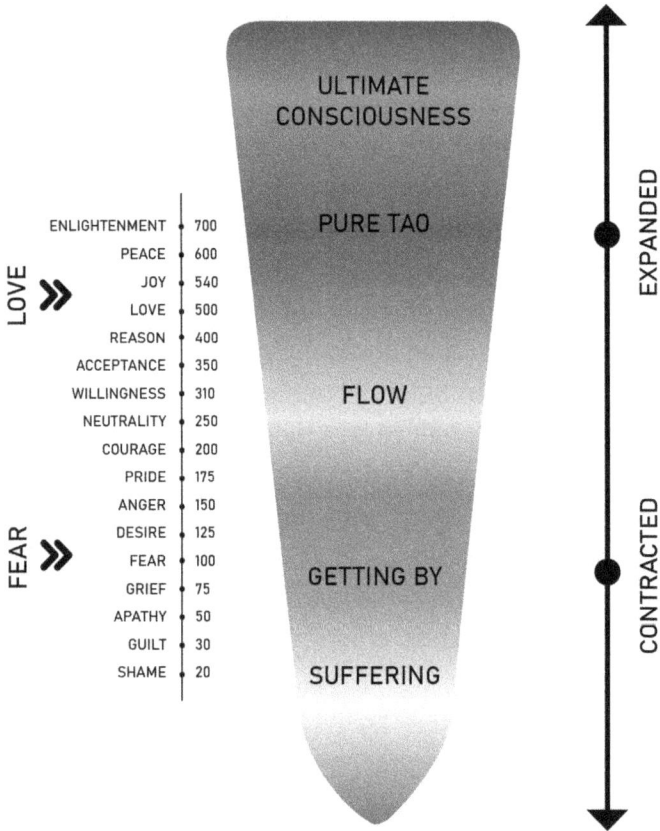

ENLIGHTENMENT	700
PEACE	600
JOY	540
LOVE	500
REASON	400
ACCEPTANCE	350
WILLINGNESS	310
NEUTRALITY	250
COURAGE	200
PRIDE	175
ANGER	150
DESIRE	125
FEAR	100
GRIEF	75
APATHY	50
GUILT	30
SHAME	20

LOVE »

FEAR »

ULTIMATE CONSCIOUSNESS

PURE TAO

FLOW

GETTING BY

SUFFERING

EXPANDED

CONTRACTED

SOURCE: HTTPS://INTUITIVELEADERSHIPMASTERY.COM/
EMOTIONAL-PHYSICAL-PAIN-ONE-HURTS/

DAVID R. HAWKINS VIBRATIONAL FREQUENCY CHART

Display Emotional Intelligence

Emotions are basically vibrational frequencies that interact with our five senses, shaping our experiences. When understood with deep awareness, they serve as guides that tell us when to shift in order to attain a more balanced state of mind. As exhibited in the chart above, emotions can range from low frequencies like anxiety, anger, and fear to higher frequencies such as joy, love, and peace.

Viewing our emotions as neither good nor bad, but rather as energies seeking forward movement, allows us to perceive them in a more constructive light. When we experience stress, anxiety, or fear, it's simply energy attempting to move through us and be released. Understanding this is crucial for personal growth. Recognizing these low vibrations enables us to acknowledge and release dense, heavy emotions, thereby maintaining a higher frequency overall.

Everything in life vibrates—our thoughts, emotions, and state of mind—shaping our natural behavior and personality. Next, we're going to look at brainwaves that will help you control the surrounding vibrations, activate your brain cells, and alter your vibration to manifest what you desire. Analyzing the vibrations around you while practicing self-care can help raise your vibration.

Now, I want to request that you make a certain lifestyle shift. First, under absolutely no circumstances can you listen to music harking back to traumatic or sad memories. In fact, even setting this aside, you can't listen to any songs that lower your frequency, as they'll set you back miles from the work we've done together! Secondly, whenever you feel a lack of a certain emotion (for example, joy when you're sad, or accomplishment when you're demotivated), refer to the chart above and look up its frequency. Then, put on some music with the same frequency. You'll find plenty of great ones online with a good search. Music is made up of sounds that are generated by waveforms whose frequency is expressed in Hertz (Hz). Isn't that simply fascinating?

Your Brain Has Waves!

Our brains are a network of neurons, buzzing with energy and emitting electrical signals. These signals essentially create brainwaves that are tied to different mental states (Dean 2020). Pascal Fries, a German scientist, explained how these electrical patterns sync up to make us feel and think different things. He focused on beta, gamma, and theta waves, each playing a role in our consciousness.

There are five types of brainwaves: gamma, beta, alpha, theta, and delta. Each type is like a different gear in the miraculous machine we call the brain, affecting how we think and feel.

- Gamma waves, at 32 to 40 Hertz, cover the whole brain and relate to higher cognitive functions.
- Beta waves, ranging from 13 to 32 Hertz, are generated when we're problem-solving and making decisions.
- Alpha waves, cruising at 8 to 12 Hertz, mean we're basically in a chill zone.
- Delta waves, the slowest at 0.1 to 4 Hertz, kick in when we're in deep sleep.
- And finally, theta waves, at 4 to 8 Hertz, are present during meditation and hypnosis. (We'll discuss theta waves in more detail shortly.)

Now, here's where it gets interesting. Understanding these brainwave frequencies is like having a superpower for your mind, which you can use to control how you feel and think. Ever tried meditating to clear your head? That's tapping into these brainwave states to reach a higher level of consciousness. Also, using affirmations and breathing techniques that sync up with these brainwave frequencies can actually make you feel happier and more at peace. But here's the catch: You've got to really believe in what you're doing for it to work. Your intentions need to be genuine for these techniques to have their full effect.

THETA State

As a hypnotherapist, the state of consciousness I'm most interested in is the theta state, which is associated with deep relaxation. It's characterized by brainwave patterns ranging from 4 to 8 Hz, which are much slower than those of the more alert alpha state and the waking beta state. In the theta state, we often experience a sense of deep relaxation, inner peace, and increased mental clarity. It's a state where the mind is calm, yet also highly receptive and open to new ideas and insights. The theta state is considered optimal for introspection, healing, and personal growth.

Tools to Raise Your Vibration

When we look closely at the concepts we've explored in this chapter—energy, vibration, frequencies, emotions, and brainwaves—we gain the power to take control. We can actively choose the frequencies we allow into our lives. We can make conscious decisions about the brainwave states we want to cultivate. By adjusting our vibration, we open the door to manifesting our desires.

Take a moment to assess the vibrations that surround you. Analyze yourself and your activities, then figure out which vibrations are helping you soar and which are dragging you down.

This is where self-care comes into play, by elevating your own vibration. But what exactly is self-care? It's about prioritizing yourself and your wellbeing, seeking experiences and people who uplift you. So, surround yourself with positivity to maintain a high vibration. Pay attention to your daily routines and identify what brings you joy. Anything that has this effect is a sign that you're already in a high vibrational state. One of the strongest things, perhaps, we can do for ourselves is understanding the beauty and value of simple breathwork (Cleveland Clinic 2023). The best things in life are free, yet we tend to value those that are expensive. Oxygen is one such free blessing. Maybe if there was a cost to it, we'd truly start counting our breaths. And so, my friends, let's breathe freely and mindfully!

Breathwork Technique

Let's explore how to prepare for meditation and activate specific brainwave frequencies. To enter a meditative state, focus on the frequencies of theta and alpha, which can be achieved through various methods, including sound frequencies.

Imagine you're setting out on a journey to a peaceful oasis within yourself. Find a cozy spot where you feel at ease, then let every cell in your body relax, from head to toe. Take a deep breath in and out for 30 seconds, feeling tranquility wash over you. Then, after a full exhalation, hold your breath for another 30 seconds, sinking deeper into calmness. Focus on your breath, inhaling and exhaling, for two more cycles, taking it slow and savoring the moment. With each inhale, expand your chest; with each exhale, gently contract. Inhale deeply through your nose 30 times, then exhale, moving your shoulders forward, emptying your stomach. Hold your breath for 20 seconds, feeling your body invigorated. Repeat this cycle once more if you wish, then return to normal breathing. For the final round, inhale deeply, count to eight, hold for eight seconds, then exhale. Repeat this eight times, feeling each breath infusing you with clarity and renewed energy. Afterward, you'll feel grounded and aware, like a newborn with the wisdom of ages.

This breathing technique is designed to elevate your vibra-tions, activating a powerful response within you. It heightens energy, awareness, and consciousness. By keeping your vibration high, you can experience a profound shift in consciousness. Did you know that techniques like cold showers or specific breathing exercises can shock your system, opening your aura?

During my journey, I delved into silent meditation, which helped me manage my anger and discover inner peace. I realized that emotions like anger are a choice and can be addressed through practice and self-reflection. By understanding the root of these emotions, we can transform our mindset and elevate our vibration.

Practicing techniques such as yoga, meditation, and Tai Chi, or even simple activities like singing in the shower, can help maintain a high frequency and vibration. It's also important to limit exposure to lower frequencies, such as excessive time on social media, and align your life with your passions and purpose.

Each morning, greet the day with love and gratitude for your soul's journey. Embrace your purpose and stay connected to the universe, nurturing a high vibration that resonates with your true self.

The Bright Light Around You

This is one of those things that are felt but can't be seen. We each have an aura. It can be described as an energy field that surrounds and penetrates the body (Feynman 1964), reflecting our physical, emotional, mental, and even spiritual states. One could say it's like an electromagnetic halo with layers corresponding to different aspects of our being. Think about your favorite celebrity. Do you like them just because of their accomplishment in their field and their good looks—or is there something about them that speaks to you? Chances are you've had a favorite for years, and although their accomplishments and looks mightn't have remained the same, something has. Maybe it's their aura, which connected you to them without even knowing them personally. That's how strong the phenomenon called 'aura' can be.

Your favorite person's unseen aura! The mysterious human aura. No, it isn't just a common term used in magazines to describe celebrities, or in books to describe a character well enough to connect them to the reader. It has scientific truth to it. Dr. Valerie Hunt once graced the halls of UCLA as Professor Emeritus in the Department of Psychological Science. She delved into the depths of this enigma, daring to measure the human energy field within the confines of her laboratory (1996). Using a high-frequency electron instrument, she recorded the field in audio and video formats. This experiment validated the existence of the aura, demonstrating that while some people can perceive it fully (and some can even hear it), others may catch only glimpses or feel its presence. This experience suggested that we're beings of light and vibration. Additionally, Dr. Hunt recorded radiation emanating from areas of the body traditionally associated with meridians, providing evidence of their activity and interaction within the body. We'll discuss this in the next chapter as we explore meridians.

The Heart Wants What It Wants

It was right before an important meeting, when I was at the brink of starting my career as an entrepreneur and I had to give a speech in front of high-value individuals—seasoned professionals who knew what they were doing. There I was, a young woman just starting out. Although I was full of passion and courage, my heart was racing. With chills down my spine, I was quite literally shivering, even sweating a little ... but it was how my heart reacted that forms my most dominant memory of that event.

The heart is aware. It almost always is.

Remarkably, the heart can anticipate and react to events before they occur, indicating a profound level of sensitivity. Research has revealed that the heart has its own nervous system, capable of sending signals to the brain independently. This communication pathway allows the heart to influence our cognitive functions and emotional responses in ways that people previously wouldn't have believed. The world we live in is currently focused on artificial intelligence—but did you know that the heart possesses its own intelligence? Or that it influences our perceptions, higher mental processes, and emotional experiences?

According to various scientific studies, the heart's neurons possess both short-term and long-term memory capabilities, as well as a sophisticated sensory capacity. The interactions between heart and brain are translated into our emotional experiences, shaping our feelings of fear, anger, joy, and appreciation.

Our heart's rhythm can become erratic during times of stress or information overload, sending disruptive signals to our brain and affecting our overall neurophysiological coherence. This can lead to a state of imbalance and cognitive dissonance.

Importantly, our emotions, particularly when amplified by the heart's magnetic field, have the potential to influence the quantum field around us, thus impacting our perception of reality. This reveals the heart as far more than just a mechanical pump; instead, it's an energy powerhouse that's profoundly connected with the universe.

Vibrations and the Heart

As we discussed earlier, the mind is a highly debatable topic among those who want to understand the very fabric of existence beyond the brain's chemical composition. If we look at one perspective, emotions weave the fabric of our being, creating ripples across the realm of our consciousness. Our thoughts are molded in return, guiding our actions. This intertwines with the passions that reside in our hearts. Through comprehending the interplay between heart and mind, we attain control over our expressions. I'd like to end this chapter by sharing techniques that have helped me harness positive influences in my life.

- Focus on appreciation, guidance, attitude, and attention to detail. When you're angry, shift your focus to kindness. Instead of dwelling on negative thoughts about others or your environment, redirect your thoughts to kindness and love. When you send out love, you're likely to receive love in return. This is a principle of cause and effect, where what you put out into the universe returns to you.
- Let these qualities of the heart influence your surroundings positively. Change your mindset to one of positivity, love, kindness, and appreciation. By doing so, you can create a more positive environment around you. It's important to stay aware of your feelings in the moment, even as we explore how the brain can sometimes send false signals.
- Focus your intentions on your heart. Imagine your breath flowing in and out of your heart, breathing slowly and deeply. This can help bring balance to your emotions. Whether you're meditating or feeling anxious or fearful, taking deep breaths can center you and help you communicate with your heart. By keeping yourself in a positive state, you can learn to block out negative energies.

These three techniques work together naturally, without needing conscious direction. Similarly, our actions can amplify the spiritual energy that flows through us.

Align yourself with positive frequencies such as love and positivity to create a more positive reality. Lower frequencies can lead to negative emotions like fear and anger. Our thoughts have the power to shape our reality by influencing the frequencies we emit. Positive thoughts create higher frequencies, acting as a bridge between the physical and intangible aspects of our existence.

Water Has Memory

Earlier, we talked about how the best things in life are free. Oxygen is one of these; another that we may take for granted is water. Although of course, clean water isn't exactly free, it's still a splendid resource that we don't value enough. Also, water has an underlying message that we're going to discover shortly.

In *The Hidden Messages in Water*, Japanese author Dr. Masaru Emoto discussed the groundbreaking concept of water consciousness:

> *'Water is the mirror that can show us what we cannot see. It is the blueprint for our reality, which can change with a single, positive thought. All it takes is faith if you're open to it.'*

> – DR. MASARU EMOTO

Dr. Emoto claims that water records information and distributes it while circulating the earth. Water molecules are sensitive to our thoughts, words, and even feelings—which makes sense, considering that humans and the Earth's surface are predominantly composed of water. Carrying either a negative or positive charge, this seemingly ordinary resource in life harbors an astonishing, yet little-known, power.

Dr. Emoto's mind-blowing experiments (Alive Water 2023) show that water's molecular structure can be altered, as it's influenced by the memory it retains. In other words, water can remember things and is influenced by thoughts and feelings. These laboratory studies reveal that water can grow in specific geometric patterns. Natural spring water, for example, associated with soothing nature, forms symmetrical, well-balanced crystals. Positive words and thoughts bring positive changes to water. These water-related experiments emphasize the significance of using water with positive energy for our own wellbeing. Conversely, water with a negatively altered structure is unsuitable for the human body, highlighting the need to treat water with love and care before drinking.

Water, humans, and planets respond to a type of energy called resonance, just as a cell phone responds to an incoming call. Both humans and water can react to different frequencies and energy. We know that the universe has vibrations, and they're created through resonance: vibration, in this case, happens when tiny units resonate with each other to confirm they exist.

So, here's another way to look at water forming different types of crystals based on whether the external conditions are soothing or chaotic: As water is exposed to resonance frequency, it forms crystals.

It's noteworthy that Dr. Emoto treated over 10,000 clients with water, successfully addressing various mental and physical health issues. His understanding that water can memorize information is supported by water crystal photography, revealing that water responds to different information vibrations by displaying distinct designs.

Consuming water while experiencing positive emotions like love enhances our wellbeing. This is why our intentions should be as pure as the water we drink. It's vital that we avoid consuming water (unless it's necessary, of course!) when we're experiencing negative emotions such as hate and anger. In this case, we know what to do—breathe!

As we conclude this chapter, I hope I've successfully explained just how crucial energy is, that everything in essence is energy. That there's literally a precise symphony of vibrations. From the very fabric of our universe operating on frequencies to the very atom of our own existence resonating with vibration, we're all connected in the most beautiful way.

Enlightenment Takeaways

Positive Energy Transformation

What are Meridians in Traditional Chinese Medicine?

First, let's reflect on what kind of 'passageways' are you familiar with.

Are they:

The school corridor that connected the biology class with the assembly hall?

Or

A hidden way connecting the rest of the house to the store-room or cellar?

Or

The corridor between the pantry and your office?

Or

That old castle in that movie with the surprisingly long walk-ways connecting one room to another?

You see where I'm taking you, right? Good. Now that you have these images in your mind, I want you to think of merid-ians as these passageways. Meridians are basically pathways in the body through which vital energy, called 'qi' (say CHEE), flows. In Traditional Chinese Medicine (TCM) and integrative medicine systems like acupuncture and acupressure, which we'll explore in a bit, meridians are seen as networks that link parts of the body (Longhurst 2010), including organs, glands, and tissues. There are specific meridians associated with different organs and func-tions in the body, and the flow of qi through these meridians is thought to be essential for maintaining health and wellbeing.

Each meridian is believed to have specific functions related to the flow of qi and the health of the associated organs. It's imperative that we understand this concept to maintain physi-cal, emotional, and spiritual wellbeing. Various practices, includ-ing acupuncture, can help achieve this balance.

Masks of an Energy Vampire

An energy vampire sucks all the positive energy out of another person, situation, experience, or even place. They siphon off positive emotions and good energy. The sad part is, they don't even use the good energy they've stolen from you for their own benefit. Do you remember when a certain Japanese saying broke the internet a while back (Nucleus AI 2024)? It says that a human being wears three masks: One at home, one for the outside world, and one that they only show to themselves. I believe that an energy vampire wears an unfavorable mask almost all of the time, and as much as it impacts others, it affects them too. Their perspective of the world naturally deters them from attracting positive experiences for themselves.

It's easy to identify an energy vampire, is it not? I'd prompt you to look deep within yourself and reflect. The easiest way is to ask yourself: *Who is it that brings me down and lowers my self-image, right after I talk to them?*

- Consider the interactions and conversations that leave you feeling drained, disheartened, or less aligned with your true self. These might be instances where you find yourself doubting your abilities, feeling emotionally depleted, or experiencing a sense of negativity after the exchange.
- Reflect on the patterns and dynamics of these encounters. Do they consistently leave you feeling uninspired or disconnected from your authentic self?

It's important to trust your intuition and emotional responses, because your heart often holds valuable insights that can help you discern whether certain individuals or interactions are draining your energy. By tuning into these signals and recognizing the patterns, you can begin to identify and address the presence of energy vampires in your life, ultimately reclaiming your emotional wellbeing and preserving your inner vitality.

Reflect on whether you are, at any instant, acting like an energy vampire. It's always good to be self-aware.

Keeping Them Away

Once we've identified people in our lives who may be acting as energy vampires, we need to also identify reasons why people act the way they do. There are ways to cultivate and improve communication with those energy vampires in our lives whom we may not be able to completely cut ourselves off from. As for mere acquaintances, by all means cut that cord—it's not serving your soul, only diminishing it. Remember, regardless of which approach you administer, kindness—both to yourself and to others—is the key to everything positive you may wish to manifest.

Here's something you can try instantly!

1. **Feel your quietude**. Imagine a crystal box that's shielding you from any external energies or words. Affirm: I'm a strong energy, and I choose to keep my energy for myself.
2. **Surround yourself with a soft white positive light**. Think of it as a protective shadow or line coming from the top.
3. **Guard your emotions**. (No need to offer explanations or details of the negative sources.)
4. **No need to feed your ego**. Instead, become fulfilled from within and imagine that your negative source is empty.

The fact is, you feel drained because you allowed someone or something to take all that happy, healthy energy from you. When it comes to saying no and setting boundaries, you must want to do so. Not because you know you should, but because you understand the benefits of protecting and feeding your own energy, as well as the consequences of always feeding someone else's. This is a difficult idea to put into practice for a lot of us, since we tend to want to help our coworkers, friends, and family more than ourselves. But the adage is true: You must love yourself first.

Enlightenment

In the previous chapter as well as this one, we focused on frequencies, vibrations, and spiritual balance, all of which have been explored by established disciplines including quantum physics and Traditional Chinese Medicine. Keeping the knowledge we've discovered close to our hearts, we'll now walk toward the liberating state of being enlightened.

The following are steps adorned with a bright light that will guide you to realizing your full potential:

1. **Identify Your Passion**: Find something you naturally excel at and feel passionate about. This could be your true calling, reflecting your innermost self. Integrate this passion into your personality.
2. **Embrace Presence**: Cultivate mindfulness and awareness of your surroundings. Appreciate the present moment and listen to your inner voice. Instead of letting external influences define you, follow your own path.
3. **Overcome Fear**: Face challenges and confront your fears. While fear is natural, it can hinder your growth and success. Calculate risks logically and use fear as a tool for self-improvement rather than a barrier.
4. **Self-Reflection and Improvement**: Spend time meditating and contemplate your future self. If you have role models, adopt their positive traits while creating your unique identity.

Address any addictions and develop constructive routines to overcome them.

5. **Let Go of Ego**: Ego can cloud your judgment and lower your vibrations. By releasing ego, you can make clearer decisions aligned with your true self. Learn to say no and understand your limitations.

6. **Focus on Strengths**: Instead of dwelling on weaknesses, leverage your strengths. Use positive affirmations and thoughts to maintain a healthy vibration. Replace negative thoughts with positive ones to shape your reality.

7. **Embrace Continuous Learning**: Enlightenment is a continuous journey, not a final destination. Embrace each experience, good or bad, as a learning opportunity. Stay connected to the present while pursuing your dreams.

The path to enlightenment involves aligning your vibrations with your true essence, embracing challenges, and continuously evolving. As we move on to the next chapter, let's take a moment to take it all in, and brace ourselves for practically manifesting the life of our dreams.

The Subconscious is Our Partner to Success

Unleash Your Potential and Overcome Obstacles

Success can mean different things to different people. If we don't understand that, not only are we lacking empathy, we're also setting impossible expectations for everyone, and that's just not fair. In the long run, this mindset makes our own goals feel far-fetched at times, and there's an air of competitiveness that lingers because we feel everyone wants what we want.

That's not what success is, though. For some, success is about being a nurturing parent, and for others it's about being well-known. There are people who feel successful once they've reached a point where they can easily help those who are deserving without having to worry about themselves.

Even if two people have the same goals, their motivations can be as different as day and night. Some people associate success with monetary rewards, wealth, and riches. That could be anyone, from a stay-at-home wife with an affluent husband to her affluent husband himself! They both want the same things, but their motivations are quite different. The wife desires financial success so her family enjoys the luxuries this world has to offer, whereas the husband wants the same things, but might not care as much about the luxuries as he does about gratification and a strong portfolio in, say, the stock market!

So, define what success means to you. Most people who are unclear about what success really means to them believe that success means an end to the problems in their lives.

The question is: Do successful people have problems?

Surely, they do. We know that. To those who don't fully comprehend the magnitude of being successful, it might feel like the problems that their future self will have won't impact them the way their current ones do. Logically, it makes complete sense. However, this logic compromises the essence of success itself.

A long-standing successful person has three undeniable traits.

- They possess an unwavering clarity of purpose.
- They're resilient in the face of adversity.
- They have an unyielding commitment to their goals.

That's the truth about a person with enduring success. Another truth is that we all want to be successful, one way or another. The challenge we face is that we feel that the path toward success is often plagued with obstacles. Some of them are real, while others are only a byproduct of our fears that may never manifest. As we strive for success, we often encounter numerous challenges that test our resolve. Only those of us who overcome them can embark on what we call the journey to success.

Success is a State of Mind

Success doesn't necessarily mean that life will be devoid of inconveniences, setbacks, and personal shortcomings. At least, that's not what enduring success can offer. When you define what success means to you, actively work toward achieving it, then strive to maintain it, you'll understand the freedom it offers. Knowing what you truly want and steering towards it will silence regret for life's unavoidable lack of perfection. Understanding your goals empowers you to achieve them, no matter the circumstances. Never surrendering, you'll use every setback as a stepping-stone to greater success.

This quest for clarity applies to everything you desire, not just those big, life-changing goals. Be clear about everything, including the nitty-gritty details. As a girl, I used to watch the 1995 cult classic *Clueless* a lot. One particular scene (and I'm sure many fashionistas would agree with me) was when the main character, the popular and fashionable high school student Cher Horowitz, displayed her wardrobe. There was just something about it that made my heart race. Years later, when I could finally design the wardrobe of my dreams, I knew exactly the essence it should have. It was all my own, and it didn't even look like Cher's, but that feeling, the kind that got my heart racing every time I saw the scene ... that feeling was a duplicate!

When your desires, passions, and life goals are clear, your true potential emerges. It isn't your fault if the concept of success has been a hazy one in the past. The concepts you hold are shaped by a lot more than just your present observations and opinions. To understand this, we must understand the subconscious.

The Subconscious and its Power

The relationship between the conscious and subconscious mind is a fascinating one. The conscious mind is where we analyze, reason, and make decisions, while the subconscious operates below awareness, shaping our automatic behaviors and emotional responses.

Our conscious beliefs influence the goals we set, decisions we make, and actions we take. The subconscious mind is a fundamental part of psychology, profoundly influencing our thoughts, feelings, and behaviors. Understanding its power can significantly impact personal development and behavioral change. If we believe in our abilities, set ambitious goals, and work consistently towards them, our subconscious aligns itself, helping us stay motivated and resilient. It is, however, easier said than done because our mind is a lot more complex than setting a few briefs into action.

This phenomenon, an empowered subconscious, is the underlying key to most successful people. I've witnessed this firsthand with clients, family members, and if I may say so, even in myself.

Let me tell you a little story. My wonderful father had a profound impact on my subconscious. When I was fifteen, I'd be wide-eyed when he would take me to work with him. His work was all about construction, tenders, and heavy-duty equipment. I never thought I'd have anything to do with all that. I'd just lounge around his workplace like his little princess, expecting to watch him do business meetings and manage his team in complete awe.

Fast-forward to today. I'm literally doing the same things in my own field, even though I never pursued civil engineering. My subconscious was storing all those experiences, and it inevitably shaped the choices I made in the future.

Many people wonder about the subconscious mind's location and how it works. It's not physically located, but profoundly shapes our experiences and behaviors. Do you ever wonder where the subconscious resides? We all know it's there ... somewhere. Where is it? Does the subconscious have close ties with your heart? After all, they say the heart wants what it wants, and the subconscious is known to possess immense power.

Of course, we also understand it's somewhere in the mind, but where exactly? Is it an emotional equivalent of what we philosophically call the 'heart'? There are many mysteries about it, but luckily, the truth is quite simple.

Let's delve into some of the most insightful facets of the subconscious. Think of your mind as a three-tiered system, as explained by Sigmund Freud in psychoanalysis. First, there's the conscious mind, which is all about your day-to-day thoughts and feelings. Then, there's the unconscious mind, where you store memories you might need for specific tasks.

But here's the deal: The subconscious mind is where the real action happens. It's arguably the most mysterious from the tier, but it holds the key to the secrets of the universe if understood correctly. The subconscious starts forming while you're still in your mother's womb, absorbing every single experience from then on. It's like a memory bank that logs everything from your early days, even when you were just a tiny baby dependent on others for survival.

Human beings are nothing short of a miracle, and this life is a beautiful gift bestowed upon us by our Creator. Did you know that unborn babies, at twenty-two weeks, begin to form a subconscious mind? The senses begin to form roughly three months before birth, which I feel is miraculous. In my interpretation, the subconscious forms so early on for the baby to be ready for their environment. That's why it's crucial for the caregivers to deliberately design surroundings that will positively impact the unborn baby, from playing happy tunes to reading words of love and affection. Most importantly, making sure the mother carrying the child is happy and her mental health is well cared for.

Fast forward to your first seven years of life—this is when your mind is a sponge, soaking in everything. Your senses are firing on all cylinders, forming the building blocks of your life. The people around you play a huge role in shaping your beliefs and behaviors during this time. They essentially write the initial chapters of the 'life manual' stored in your subconscious mind.

Your subconscious mind isn't just chilling in your brain. Nope, it's way more pervasive. Every cell in your body holds this information, creating what's called cellular memory. It's like your entire body becomes a warehouse for your subconscious mind. That's why sometimes your body seems to act on its own, almost like it has a mind of its own!

Think of all the content you're consuming on a daily basis. Yes, I use the word 'content', because isn't it the most underused word in the 21st century? (Kidding.) Think about the posts on social media, the ads you come across, the conversations you overhear when you're not actively listening, and even the random sounds and colors you encounter. We absorb those things even when we don't intend to. Do we absorb it all? Not really. Our subconscious mind usually takes in what moves us emotionally. That could be any emotion—fascination, fear, love, grief, etc. Even memories from childhood—associations with certain sounds, for example—can stir us in the present. They can sometimes be negative, like a glass breaking during a fight, or positive, like the sound of your classmates clapping as you receive an award in school. These associations are very much a force in your present, and being aware of them helps keep things in perspective.

But here's the twist: Your subconscious mind doesn't always align with your conscious desires. It's like having two horses pulling your life in different directions, which can make achieving your goals feel like an uphill battle.

Let's say your conscious mind strives for a goal. And then our subconscious mind comes along, instilling fear through adapted patterns and acquired information that doesn't align with your goal. This is where hypnosis, a practice still not fully understood by many, comes into play by reprogramming your subconscious at your own behest. We'll dive deep into hypnosis in the next chapter.

But fear not! There are ways to reprogram this powerhouse called the subconscious mind. Your subconscious mind is like a superhero working behind the scenes. By understanding it and tweaking its programming, you can steer your life in the direction you want. It's like fine-tuning a high-performance engine—once you've got it running smoothly, you're all set for an accelerated journey towards your goals! To help understand more about it, let's take a deep dive into the first seven years of life, and how they shape the subconscious mind.

The First Seven Years

This is a concept that's been around since time immemorial, but only recently gained the momentum it deserves. A child's early experiences, surroundings, and interactions shape their subconscious beliefs, perceptions, and behavioral patterns. These subconscious programs can have a profound impact on a child's development, influencing their self-image, beliefs about the world, and potential for success and happiness. Without further deliberate intervention, chances are that these seven years form the foundation of an adult's present life. Therefore, it's crucial to understand and support children in shaping better lives for themselves as they grow and mature. Understanding this concept will also help you apply tools to steering your ideas, hopefully reprogramming your own subconscious in the process.

Children are highly impressionable, and their subconscious minds are constantly absorbing information from their environment. This information comes from interactions with family members, peers, media, and societal structures. These early experiences can form the foundation of a child's beliefs about themselves and the world, ultimately influencing their thoughts, emotions, and actions as they navigate through life.

As an NLP (Neuro-Linguistic Programming) practitioner, I'd like to share an observation about major sense representations that could be useful to you:

- Visual (images)
- Auditory (sounds)
- Kinesthetic (touch and internal feelings).

Each of us has certain senses that are more dominant than others, or stimulants for each sense which move us more strongly than others. For example, the scent of lavender might move some of us very positively by instilling calmness, while a picture of lavender might not trigger the same emotion (or vice versa). By identifying a child's dominant senses, we can help create positive surroundings that they'll respond strongly to. (For example, happy or serene music helps create a strong auditory sense.)

When children are exposed to negativity, criticism, or limited opportunities, their subconscious programming may lead them to develop beliefs of unworthiness, fear, or self-doubt. Conversely, when children are nurtured, supported, and provided with positive reinforcement, their subconscious programming can instill beliefs of confidence, resilience, and optimism.

Given the profound impact of subconscious programming on a child's development, it's safe to say that as parents, caregivers, educators, and members of society, we should actively support and nurture young minds. This also gives us a splendid chance to reprogram our own subconscious to achieve our goals for a happier life. When we're aware of our environment and acquired patterns, we're better able to assess which elements to keep and which to get rid of.

Here are five of the many ways we can do this:

1. **Positive Reinforcement**: Encouraging positive behavior and accomplishments. By acknowledging efforts and achievements, we can help ourselves and others develop a positive self-image. Positive affirmations are a beautiful way to do this, instilling a sense of security.

2. **Providing a Nurturing Environment**: Creating a safe and supportive environment for ourselves and others. When we feel safe and loved, we're more likely to develop a sense of security.

3. **Understanding Emotional Intelligence**: Understanding and managing our emotions is important for overall wellbeing, which involves learning how to express feelings in healthy ways and coping with challenges. We can empower ourselves and others to navigate life's ups and downs more effectively.

4. **Challenging Limiting Beliefs:** Identifying and addressing limiting beliefs that we may have internalized is essential. By

creating opportunities to challenge these beliefs and explore new possibilities, we can expand our vision and help others do the same.

5. **Encouraging Critical Thinking**: When we think critically and question the world around us, we foster a sense of curiosity and empowerment. By encouraging ourselves and others to explore different perspectives, we can help them develop a strong sense of self and community.

The Stubborn Part of Your Mind

Reprogramming the subconscious to your own benefit sounds intriguing … until you come face to face with parts of your mind that have acquired old patterns that deter you. Understanding the root causes of this stubbornness often requires a deliberate and introspective approach. There are several steps you can take to gain insight into the underlying reasons behind this behavior. First and foremost, self-reflection is crucial. Take a moment to ponder over instances where evidence of stubbornness can offer valuable clues. Consider the triggers, thoughts, and emotions that accompany these situations. Delve deeper into any recurrent themes associated with this behavior to unveil patterns.

Exploring one's past is equally significant. Reflect upon your upbringing and significant relationships. Assess whether certain events or influences from the past might have contributed to the development of stubborn tendencies. Childhood experiences and family dynamics can significantly shape behavioral patterns, warranting self-reflection regarding their potential influence.

Moreover, examining the underlying emotions linked to stubbornness is imperative. Emotions like fear, insecurity, or the desire for control often underpin stubborn behaviors. Analyzing how these emotions relate to personal experiences and beliefs can better explain the driving forces behind such behavior.

Assessing personal beliefs and values is also crucial. It's important to ponder whether stubbornness is rooted in deeply ingrained beliefs or values. Reflect on whether these convictions serve a constructive purpose, or if they contribute to stubborn behavior that no longer proves beneficial.

Identifying triggers is another pivotal step. Being mindful of specific circumstances or interactions that tend to provoke stubbornness can provide valuable insights into its root causes. Understanding these triggers is key to comprehending the deeper reasons behind such behavioral patterns.

Finally, if stubbornness significantly impacts relationships, work, or overall wellbeing, seeking professional help is advisable. Consulting a therapist or counselor can offer a structured approach to delve into the underlying causes of stubbornness. They can provide guidance and support in developing more adaptive coping strategies tailored to individual needs.

By engaging in self-reflection, seeking external perspectives, and considering various factors contributing to stubbornness, one can gain a deeper understanding of its underlying causes. This heightened awareness can serve as a catalyst for positive change, facilitating the development of more flexible and adaptive approaches to challenges and interactions. Moving forward, let's talk about how we can shift old patterns into constructive habits.

Unleash Your Potential and Overcome Obstacles

A paradigm is basically the lens through which you see things. If your vision is blurry, or the lens power isn't correct, you may not be able to unleash your potential. Doing a complete paradigm shift can help unleash our potential and overcome obstacles. Here's a quick checklist that will help put things in perspective.

1. Recognize and challenge existing beliefs to gain clarity and understanding of one's perspectives and biases for a transformative shift.
2. Believe that you can redesign your mindset to one that serves you.
3. Envision yourself with new habits and hone your skills.
4. Deliberately define clear, purpose-driven objectives.
5. Cultivate an approach of patience and endurance.

It's Time for Positive Change

Mind Mechanics

Make the Change Now

It's usually when a crisis arises that we become determined to switch things up in our life. Why wait? Why not steer a change that might even avoid that crisis in the first place? I understand that as humans, one of our strongest motivations can be a challenge. But … imagine possessing a mindset that's ever-so-grateful for God's blessings. After all, who else are you going to turn to? It's God, and God alone. If you're interested in the Law of Attraction, you probably know what a huge emphasis it places on gratitude. You might think that wanting change and being grateful come into conflict with one another, but that's far from the truth. When you're in an abundant mindset, you're grateful and focus on your blessings. This mindset continues to extend in terms of your goals. You see your goals as blessings, not physical or mental hurdles you have to pass through.

Choose the life you desire now—you have the power to transform it into one filled with joy, health, and inspiration. Instead of passively waiting for change, proactively pursue it. Stop merely predicting outcomes and take charge of shaping the life you envision. We can initiate change by altering our mindset. We can replace negative thoughts with positive ones through self-awareness. Our minds shape our reality in numerous ways, and the thoughts we harbor greatly influence our lives. Begin dismantling each negative, toxic thought pattern by consciously challenging it.

When I think about my master, Beryl Comar, I'm filled with gratitude for everything that she's taught me. I discovered how my mind works, and her knowledge of NLP helped steer my understanding to more insightful realms. She's a leader in her field of using suggestive techniques to get over severe anxiety. Her success in helping people overcome their phobia of going to the dentist has been phenomenal. Her prowess in NLP,

EFT (Emotional Freedom Techniques), and other approaches to helping adults and children overcome their fears has been transformational (Medical News Today 2019). I'll cherish her treasure-trove of knowledge, as I know it will continue with me until my last breath.

Beryl introduced me to the following affirmation: Every day, I get better, and better, and better, and better. I continue adding the word 'better' repeatedly depending on how grateful I feel; I promise there are usually a lot of 'betters'. Do that now and see if it switches your emotional gear even slightly. I sincerely hope it does.

Shifting immediately from negative repeated thoughts can be challenging, but there are techniques that can help interrupt and redirect those thoughts in the moment.

Awareness

Being aware is the key to abruptly halting your negative thoughts. It begins with identifying that your thoughts are going in the wrong direction, then instantly implementing the willpower to do something about them.

Stop Now.

Call out: 'Stop!' or 'Cancel!'

Say it loud if you can.

Say it in your mind if you can't say it loud.

But say it to yourself, regardless.

This puts a vocal halt to your negative thought cycle, providing a momentary pause to redirect your focus.

You are in control of your thoughts, and your thoughts should never be in control of you. You are stronger than your thoughts; use it to your advantage.

Visualization

You've called out 'stop' to a negative thought, and now it's time to visualize the same, making the emotion even stronger. Picture a stop sign or a red light in your mind when negative thoughts occur. Then, intentionally shift your focus to a positive mental image or scenario that brings you joy or peace.

Another thing I like to do is imagine a magnificent white cloud, full of glory and goodness, which begins raining positive thoughts. Those positive thoughts fill my body with a beautiful calmness.

Redirect Attention—Pattern

Shift your focus onto positive aspects when negative thoughts emerge, employing techniques like breathwork or engaging in activities that bring joy or peace. Patterns play an important role. We may not even know them, but we experience patterns in our daily lives. Obvious examples include your daily routine, while less obvious ones include your decision-making habits, your spending habits, your response to certain triggers, etc. Some are good patterns, and some aren't. Make a list of all your identifiable patterns and compartmentalize them into good and bad. This will help you gain insight into how these patterns affect you. Next, shift to the positive patterns every time you have negative thoughts. You can choose from your list, and even create new ones to follow.

Positive Affirmations and Prayer

As I mentioned earlier, I keep repeating this: Every day, I get better, and better, and better. This is an affirmation (Cascio et al 2016). Positive affirmations counter negative thoughts instantly.

Repeat empowering statements like 'I'm capable and resilient', 'I choose positivity', or 'I have the ability to shape my thoughts and actions'. These affirmations help reframe your mindset towards optimism and strength. With affirmations comes gratitude, and with gratitude comes prayer. Prayer is one of the strongest forms of affirmation, because you not only affirm a positive output, but also surrender to a higher power with complete confidence.

It's important to recognize that these techniques may not work instantly for everyone, and may require practice and persistence to become effective. If negative thoughts persist and significantly impact your wellbeing, consider seeking professional help from a therapist or counselor.

You may have noticed that a lot of the above is directly leading toward prayer. Since I believe in God, I believe that all my manifestations are a mercy from him, and I'm eternally grateful for each one of them. Believing in a higher power isn't only spiritually soothing; the concept taps right into the logical side of our brains. How? Here's an example. When we naturally want something with all our might, it isn't easily attainable in our minds. Do we have the power to manifest it in tangible or quantifiable form immediately, within a second? Chances are, for most of us that's a plain 'no'. Believing in a higher power helps put our minds to rest. That there's a God with that kind of power. That if we pray for it with clean intent and undeniable faith, it will manifest.

As I've mentioned earlier, humans are miraculous beings. The human mind has been studied extensively, yet nobody fully knows how it works. That's the beauty of God's creation—it can't be fully understood because we don't have the knowledge He does. However, God has blessed us with more knowledge than His other creations. We have a complex mind and we've been given the honor of free will. It is, then, completely up to us to make something positively inspiring out of our cognitive complexities.

Positive Patterns and Mental Filters

You need the awareness that your mind is just another part of your body, like your limbs and eyes (Tu et al 2022). It can trick you, shooting forth signals and thoughts that aren't always going to work in your favor. Therefore, when we think of something positive, we're creating patterns or pathways in our brains; eventually, our thought process becomes a pattern.

An old friend had an unfortunate pattern in her life: She would continually attract partners who were inclined to cheat. There were many complex reasons behind that, but she consequently developed a bias which translated into her opinion of all men. To say the least, this was unfair to the people around her—and even more to herself, because it got in the way of her finding a faithful partner. Rest assured, she's very happy now, has manifested the man of her dreams, and continues reaching out to me about her beautiful progress. (It's always a work in progress.)

Now, we've all heard of the placebo effect. When you're unwell, the doctor could prescribe a medicine that might not actually help physically. But if you believe it will, even if it's just made of sugar, that belief can speed up your recovery. It might sound odd, but lots of experiments prove this. That's why you often see positive folks leading positive lives—how you think really matters.

The placebo effect is a real motivation booster, showing how powerful the mind is. And you know what? It's not always a bad thing! In fact, if we're smart about it, we can use the placebo effect to our advantage. But there's a flip side called the 'nocebo effect'—when there's a negative impact. Take a look at the news. There's so much negativity, and it can put us off. But how is that empowering us? What empowers us is knowledge. So, instead of falling into the nocebo trap, consider: Why might that bad news be important?

The nocebo effect results in negative thinking, which tires the mind. Imagine expecting the worst by making negative assumptions—then, once the worst manifests, going through that suffering again in reality. It isn't worth it. Don't let that person tell you that you're going to fail that test because apparently that teacher doesn't like you. And yes, that was true of someone close to me. No, don't let others play with your mind.

The pandemic in 2020 changed everything and everyone, forever. For me, it started out as a shocker—but when I took a step back and looked at my life's story during this chaotic time, I realized something amazing. I felt grateful. Surprisingly, this tough period allowed me to connect deeply with God, reconnect with my inner self, and spend quality time with my family. Those moments of peace and quiet made me realize what's truly important to me. Now, I feel this urge to share what I've learned with people who might be struggling or feeling a bit lost in their daily lives. There's something about this experience that made me want to reach out and help those who need it most.

Watch your thoughts and be aware of the ongoing self-talk in your mind.

Be mindful of how you think. Why? Because your life is shaped by your thoughts. Be careful how you think. Because what you think shapes your life.

Self-Healing

Sometimes you have to shift the way you see things in your mind and change how you perceive things. It's kind of like giving the pictures in your head a new frame to fit into. Naturally, this shall involve releasing negative emotions and limiting beliefs linked to past experiences. The goal is to facilitate long-term change and enhance overall mind–body health.

We are going to do a technique that aims at reflecting on past events and utilizing them as a resource for creating a positive future. Let's immerse.

Imagine yourself seated in a theater, observing the screening of your life's movie.

Become a silent observer.

Take a reflective journey back to each year of your life, beginning from your current age.

Identify the most important events during that stage.

Stop where there's resistance.

Confront yourself where there's resistance.

Confront the people who influenced it profoundly. (Good and bad.)

Remember, speak to them and yourself in the third person.

Hug yourself. Offer compassion and healing for yourself through each challenging experience.

No need to rush this: Allow yourself the necessary time; there's no rush to complete this introspection in a single session.

After traversing through your past, transition to creating a future timeline. Envision the potential path ahead, visualizing the opportunities, aspirations, and goals that form a narrative for your forthcoming chapters. Think about the kind of life you truly desire. Picture the body shape you've always wanted, consider the type of work that genuinely excites you, and identify what you're naturally good at.

Mind Power and Emotional Intelligence (Hypnosis)

Today is a great day

Yesterday was full of experience

Tomorrow, the best will come, and I shall not worry because it is for God to know.

Before we begin talking about hypnosis, I'd like to say something. We alone possess the power and responsibility to initiate our healing journey—others can only assist (Cherry 2024).

The concept of a 'healer' isn't exclusive; in reality, you're the architect of your own destiny. Embrace the understanding that your ability to heal and transform your life lies within you, guiding the course of your own healing process. Even those recognized as healers require healing themselves; no profession reaches completion without ongoing learning and growth.

Now, hypnosis is basically a hyper-focused state where you're fully involved (Mayo Clinic 2024), like when you get lost in the thrill of a suspense movie and temporarily forget that it's just a movie. It's like entering a make-believe world.

When you're in this state, you pause your usual judgments and tap into powers you might not realize you had. It's like suddenly noticing habits or movements you didn't even know you were doing until someone points them out—pretty neat, huh?

Your brain's a wizard at filtering sensations—deciding what's important and what's not. And guess what? We can learn to control and use this power.

People often mess up the idea of hypnosis, thinking it's about losing control, but it's actually a way to gain control and find hidden aspects of yourself.

It's all about looking at things differently. If you're feeling pain, for example, your brain's getting signals from your body—but how you interpret those signals varies based on whether you're scared or in pain. You could react the same way to the same pain signals, unless you flex your mind a bit and choose to see them differently.

Hypnosis isn't a therapy all by itself; it's more like super-concentration. You have to pair it with a strategy to get those therapeutic benefits.

Your subconscious mind is like a guard—it's there to protect you. Not only this, but your subconscious can also help you pave the right path for yourself. Not too long ago, I suggested hypnosis to my niece. She was at a crossroads, not knowing what career path to choose. Both her options were as different as day and night. I conducted a hypnosis session, sieved through all that cognitive bias stopping her from assuming her full potential, and bam! She knew what she wanted, and with that clarity came an opportunity. She was chosen for a prestigious school among only nine other candidates worldwide, going on to secure an internship in one of the world's biggest production firms.

Right before falling asleep, and usually also when you're waking up, your mind is in theta. It's the best time to visualize positive outcomes. In my interpretation, it's the soul that arrives first each day as you wake up; by checking social media or letting negative thoughts enter our mind, we're doing it a disservice. Engage in a conversation with your inner self before immersing yourself in external distractions. Your soul deserves that. Also, you can activate heightened awareness and consciousness within your daily routine. I switch up things, for instance. Sometimes I'll use my right hand to brush my teeth, and sometimes my left. The same applies to waking up on a certain side. The small things, you know? This aims for balanced cognition. (Also, it's kind of fun.)

I'd like to share the Confusing Technique for self-hypnosis with you. It's a play-on-words-and-get-into-theta kind of a thing. With congruent breathwork, start counting backward from one hundred. Since your mind isn't used to counting backward, it will get confused; a point will come when you'll enter the theta state of deep relaxation. Once you're there, ask yourself a question. (It's advisable to have already thought about the question or goal beforehand.) Make sure, please, that the question or goal is affirming the positive, not the negative. For example:

- A negative question is: Why isn't it working out for me?
- A positive question is: How should I make it work?

As we progress to yet another chapter, I'd like to express my gratitude to you for continuing on this journey with me, and hope that you manifest the life of your dreams by shedding further light on emotional intelligence.

Manifesting Your Desires

The Laws

What's stopping you?

The universe is complicated from the outside, and simple when it's within you.

Let's skip to the good part. We'd better make sure all the little parts of our lives are the 'good' parts. It's time to discuss the very thing that's made you hang around—but first, I'd like to extend my gratitude. Thank you.

Thank you for continuing on this journey with me. Let's take a deep breath, wish everyone luck in their endeavors, and manifest our best lives.

This chapter emphasizes the importance of maintaining a positive frequency to align with the Law of Attraction. It explains that the Law of Attraction is constantly working, drawing into our lives experiences and circumstances matching our dominant thoughts and emotions. The chapter highlights the role of confidence, belief, and prayer in manifestation, emphasizing the power of these practices in directing our intentions towards the universe, God, or Mother Earth. It suggests that even individuals who are agnostic or non-believers can benefit from these practices, as the principles of manifestation are based on mindset and the alignment of thoughts and emotions with desired outcomes. Overall, the chapter encourages readers to cultivate a mindset of positivity and belief in the possibility of achieving their desires, regardless of their specific belief system.

We'll explore the simplicity of manifestation and the magnitude of the universe that has boundless possibilities: If only we have faith. That's also one thing we'll do a deep dive into: The faith to keep going. We'll learn to implement simple techniques and universal laws. We'll learn to combat the experiences of failure in our attempts to manifest. And, thus, we'll manifest.

Then … What's stopping you?

When you find yourself in possession of all the necessary tools but still unable to move forward, it can be a frustrating and perplexing experience. Despite having everything required to progress, there seems to be a barrier preventing you from taking the next step. This situation often arises when there are internal obstacles such as fear, self-doubt, or a lack of clarity about your goals. Via introspection, it's essential to identify these underlying issues and address them effectively.

We can go on and on about manifesting our best lives, and yet be completely clueless about how to do that. What is manifestation in its literal sense? Before we explore that question, allow me to share a little story. It's about a discussion I had a while back with a friend of mine, who was once a naysayer of the Law of Attraction.

A Life-Changing Exchange

As we sat across from each other in our favorite café, the topic of manifestation sparked a healthy debate between my friend and me. She leaned back in her chair, sipping her coffee thoughtfully, and remarked, 'All this manifestation stuff is really just senseless. It feels like it's just become a buzzword, thrown around without real substance. A thing to sell fake hope'.

I knew where she was coming from, and it wasn't a happy place. Life hadn't been easy on her, so I listened intently, nodding knowingly as she expressed her skepticism. I could understand her point of view—in a time saturated with self-help masters, life coaches, and influencers touting the power of manifestation, it's easy to become doubtful.

'I get what you're saying,' I replied, swirling my own cup of coffee. 'But I think there's more to it than just a trendy catchphrase. Manifestation is a way of life. A life with clear intention that aligns with your actions or ... well, the other way round.'

'Yes, but at the end of the day it's all about positive thinking and expecting magic to happen, right? And it's like half the world is now online and talking about manifestation … it's the internet's new favorite word … it's annoying! These are only a few people who got lucky and then they decided to make money off this new trend.'

I smiled. 'When you say, these are only a handful of people who got lucky … you mean half the world, right?'

'Razan!' My friend laughed. 'Nobody can win an argument with you.'

'Hey, I used your own words and steered them positively!' I giggled. 'And this isn't an argument, my dear. All these people sharing their stories about manifestation … How is that a bad thing? We don't bat an eyelid when we talk about negative things like … well … the news. Nobody ever said, "Oh these international news channels only talk about what's wrong in the world and it's such a wasteful trend." Then, why are we pointing at people who want to help share their wisdom?'

My friend raised an eyebrow, clearly intrigued by my perspective. 'So, you're saying it's not just luck?'

'Exactly,' I affirmed. 'It's about cultivating a mindset that empowers you to take action by making choices that lead you closer to your desires. When you truly believe in something and work towards it with determination, you're more likely to see results. Manifestation is a lifestyle.'

As we continued our conversation, I could sense my friend's negative outlook taking a turn for the better. While she may have started off dismissing manifestation as a mere buzzword, our discussion had given her a new perspective. And for me, it was a reminder that even in a world full of trends and fads, some ideas still hold weight when examined with an open mind.

Finding yourself in possession of all the necessary tools, but still unable to move forward, can be a frustrating and perplexing experience. Despite having everything required to progress, there can seem to be a barrier preventing you from taking the next step. This situation often arises when there are internal obstacles such as fear, self-doubt, or a lack of clarity about your goals. It's essential to identify these underlying issues to address them effectively.

The statement 'I'm not lucky' is a common refrain, particularly when considering matters like winning the lottery. Some individuals believe in the power of numbers and engage in practices like repeatedly imagining themselves winning. While it's true that there are people who do win the lottery, attributing their success solely to luck might overlook the aspects of strategy, statistical probability, and sheer chance involved in such games. Belief in the power of positive thinking and visualization can be beneficial, but it's important to maintain a balanced perspective rather than relying solely on luck or magical thinking.

Success is often viewed as a personal achievement, but it can also be seen as a contribution to others. When you achieve success, you have the potential to inspire and uplift those around you. This ripple effect can create a positive atmosphere fostering further success, leading to a domino effect of positive vibrations. By focusing on creating abundance that spreads beyond your individual sphere, you not only enhance your own life but also contribute to a larger cycle of positivity and growth.

The Laws

Law of Attraction

The Law of Attraction is an overused term in today's time. (I'm sure you've heard of it before.) It gained popularity through books like *The Science of Getting Rich* by Wallace D. Wattles and *The Secret* by Rhonda Byrne. It could, however, be something you don't fully understand. I've worked on a definition that I feel is easy to comprehend and relate to.

The Law of Attraction is a universal law. It means that your thoughts are shaping your experiences; positive thoughts bring about positive experiences, while negative thoughts lead to negative ones.

The key principles making up the Law of Attraction are:

1. Like Attracts Like
    Similar things are drawn to each other. Just like people tend to attract those who are like-minded, our thoughts attract corresponding outcomes.

2. There's Always Space
    This idea suggests that because it isn't possible to have a completely empty space in your mind or life, you should fill it with positive thoughts. By removing negative aspects from your life, you create space for positive things to come in. It's based on the belief that there's always something filling the void, so it's crucial to fill it with positivity.

3. A Perfect Present
    This principle focuses on the idea that there's always room for improvement in the present. Instead of dwelling on flaws, the focus is on finding ways to make the present the best it can be.

Law of Assumption
Neville Goddard is one of history's most quoted people on the Law of Attraction. He was a huge proponent of another concept known as the Law of Assumption. This means that if you truly think and act as if your desired outcome has already been accomplished, it has a higher chance of becoming reality. This

idea encourages you to fully embrace your future self, the one you'd like to manifest.

The Law of Assumption requires not just believing, but also feeling and behaving, as if you've already achieved what you desired. This has transformed many people's lives, because it shifts their focus from wanting something to actually embodying its presence. By assuming the reality of your desired outcome, you align your thoughts, emotions, and actions—thus, you manifest.

Neuroplasticity

Our thoughts and emotions have the remarkable ability to shape the structure and function of our brains. When we engage in repeated patterns of thinking or feeling, our brain forms neural pathways associated with those thoughts or emotions. This hardwires our brain to be more inclined towards those patterns in the future. Proponents of the Law of Attraction and manifestation have believed this from time immemorial. Thankfully, we now have the concept of neuroplasticity to vouch for it.

According to this idea, the brain is a dynamic organ which is fully capable of learning new behaviors and habits. The brain's structure and capacity aren't fixed! The inspiring research behind it has been conducted by notable figures including Dr Michael Merzenich, known as the 'father of neuroplasticity'. Dr. Michael Merzenich is the brain behind BrainHQ and the author of *Soft-Wired: How the New Science of Brain Plasticity Can Change Your Life*. For nearly five decades, he's been a pioneer in brain plasticity research.

This concept has explored a new dimension in improving learning, physical rehabilitation, mental illnesses, and addiction. As we've explored deeply in this book, this neuroplasticity backs up our idea that the brain can influence a person's experiences and outcomes. It implies that the brain is adaptable and can change in response to new experiences and information, so with positive effort, we can rewire it (and therefore our experience). Yes, you have the ability to rewire your brain by consciously directing your thoughts and behaviors towards specific goals or outcomes. If you practice gratitude consistently, your brain will become more attuned to positive aspects of your life, naturally leading to an overall surge in positive experiences. That's not me saying it. It's the law. The Law of Attraction.

Conditions for Success

Two Instances Where Manifestation Won't Work
The Law of Attraction is a powerful force that's gained attention for its ability to shape our lives based on our thoughts, beliefs, and intentions. However, there are certain conditions where this law may not seem to deliver the desired outcomes.

Two of these conditions stand out:

1. When we envy what others possess instead of focusing on what we want.
2. When we wish harm upon others.

Let's explore these through the lens of a fictional story.

Sarah's a talented young professional who's excellent at what she does. However, she continually harbors envy towards her colleague, Alex. From Sara's viewpoint, Alex effortlessly garners opportunities and acclaim in their workplace, and doesn't deserve the recognition he gets. She continually measures her progress against his, neglecting to leverage her own strengths to her advantage. Despite her attempts to visualize her dream workplace, Sarah's efforts are in vain. She invests a large amount of time envying what Alex has, instead of using his success as inspiration to do better. (After all, she's brilliant herself.)

Now here's what we can understand from this story in relation to the Law of Attraction. If Sarah begins to understand how the Law of Attraction works, she'll realize the importance of positive intentions and gratitude. By acknowledging her own blessings, she'd be astounded by the potential within her that she hasn't yet explored. Reflecting on her mindset and gaining awareness of her own being will help her channel her envy of Alex into inspiration to do better. It will help her realize her unique path toward success and recognition. As she focuses on what she wants, her fixation on negative emotions like destitution and envy shall begin to fade.

The takeaway is that every time she envies Alex, she inadvertently sends out signals of lack and scarcity to the universe, which in turn attracts more of the same into her life. Now, let's assume that Sarah's decided to shift her mindset with the above information.

Determined to alter her perspective, Sarah decides to focus on cultivating a mindset of abundance and gratitude. Instead of comparing herself to Alex, she begins to celebrate his successes with him! This not only helps shift her mindset toward optimism, but also makes Alex appreciate her, creating a loop of gratitude and positivity. Sarah now begins to appreciate her own strengths and accomplishments, recognizing that she has unique talents and qualities deserving her time and attention.

As Sarah's mindset shifts, she notices a change in her circumstances. Opportunities that previously eluded her begin to present themselves, and she finds herself experiencing a newfound sense of confidence and fulfillment. By releasing her envy and embracing a mindset of abundance, Sarah aligns herself with the positive energy of the Law of Attraction, allowing her to attract the success she's always desired.

Through this anecdote, we can see how the Law of Attraction is also influenced by our thoughts and intentions towards others. When we envy what others have (instead of being inspired to do better and be better) or when we wish harm upon them, we're sending out negative vibrations that can hinder our own success and wellbeing. Even when we seem to find success with such a way forward, it wouldn't be a wholesome life of abundance. Instead, it's a short-term way to success. It's a success for the world, but it's still a failure in the spiritual and human realms. When we realize that we're light, it awakens our awareness and helps us be kinder and more empathetic, opening limitless possibilities to abundance.

Conversely, when we cultivate a mindset of abundance, gratitude, and goodwill towards others, we align ourselves with the positive energy of the universe, opening the door to greater opportunities and fulfillment in our own lives.

Speaking of anecdotes, I've got another one which is close to my heart. I want to share with you the story of how I manifested my dream house. I hope it serves as an inspiration to you, so that you believe in carving out your own unique dream visions in great detail and with pure love.

Manifestation of My Dream House

My vision was quite extraordinary. I dreamed of a beautiful house, spacious yet cozy, within a close-knit community of cafés, farmers markets, and parks. The designer inside me also yearned for the architecture to be sleek, symmetrical, and predominantly made of glass! Imagine that. I thought of every detail, from solar panels right down to the horse-riding field. Finding a place like that in Dubai was unimaginable a few years ago, yet I just knew it was out there.

When I finally intended to buy my dream house years later, I looked at hundreds of houses and didn't feel a connection with any of them. I almost gave up ... until one fine moment, there it was in the blink of an eye. My friend took me to a community to meet someone, and we met the landlord who sold me the house! Just like that.

I knew every detail about my house, believing it was out there somewhere. Do your part, and let God and His universe lead you to the rest.

Find Your Own Connection

Before you do the next and final steps to live your best life, I want to share a last anecdote with you about how I came to harmonize my work identity with my core. After all, at the core, it's about finding a connection from within that resonates with all of you—the world inside you, and the world outside.

My family background in the field of construction and my love for design beautifully harmonized with my individual method of manifestation. To me, it's the same as setting something in concrete.

- You set a clear intention (feel it happening for yourself). To me this involves knowing that this is a project I want to build.
- You visualize it. To me, this involves visualizing how it will be built, along with how it will look once it's built.
- You write it down. To me, this involves getting the 3D illustrations and execution plan.
- You build it. To me, this means literally constructing a building or exhibition platform from the ground up.

To you, it could be something entirely different. You could be a doctor, finding a connection from within your methods on how you systematically treat patients. Or you could be an influencer, finding a connection from how you begin creating content from scratch. You could be a mother, finding a connection from your own style of nurturing.

I've given you the framework.

It's your turn now.

Find that connection.

Manifest Your Best Life

To manifest your desires, you need to understand the principles of intention and belief. Intention is the purpose behind your actions, the driving force that propels you towards your goals. It involves the conscious decision to focus your thoughts, emotions, and actions on a specific outcome. Belief, on the other hand, is the conviction that what you desire is not only possible but also attainable. It's the foundation upon which manifestation is built, shaping your reality based on your thoughts and expectations.

In this book, the subjects I chose to explore with you were intentional propellers toward your final manifestation. We'll look back at its content quickly, actively manifesting our best lives while doing so.

• Intention and belief

Listen to your inner voice. Know what you want, in as much detail as you want.

• Visualize in detail

Your visions are the lights that travel faster than your thoughts. Know that your vision is possible and you're deserving of it. Believe in the process.

- Where your energy goes, your manifestation flows.
- Grab the opportunity when it manifests. Do what's necessary for your dreams to materialize.
- Redirect your words and focus on what you want, rather than what you dislike.

Engage in purposeful prayer or meditation to align your consciousness with your intentions. Use these practices to connect with the universe or your higher self, seeking guidance and support in manifesting your desires. Be open to receiving signs and messages that may guide you towards your goals. By staying attuned to your inner wisdom and the universal flow of energy, you can actively shape your destiny through conscious intention.

Mastering manifestation requires a deep understanding of intention and belief. By clarifying your intentions, cultivating belief, surrounding yourself with positivity, practicing self-love, and embracing purposeful prayer and consciousness, you can harness the power of manifestation to create the life you desire. Remember that your thoughts and beliefs shape your reality, so choose them wisely and align them with your highest aspirations.

Wake Up Now

Redesign Your Life

It's a surreal feeling that our journey together is now coming to an end. The good part is, you can keep this book on your shelf, hopefully somewhere within reach, and come back to it often. Oh, I sincerely hope that you do; that way, we can keep meeting. Manifestation, at the end of the day, is a lifelong journey. I myself have to consult some of my own findings at times. As human beings, we tend to forget things. That's why books are so magical. They stay with us, helping us get by in difficult times. As we move forward, we must continue nurturing our dreams, believing in ourselves and our abilities, and taking inspired action towards our goals. We must remain open to the opportunities that present themselves and have faith.

Wake Up Now isn't just a project to me—it's a profound journey that resonates deeply with my soul. It's about igniting a fire within, exposing every part of our being to the incredible possibilities life has to offer. It's about awakening the earnestness for knowledge, awakening our senses to the beauty around us, and awakening our lives to the vastness of the universe. I wholeheartedly believe in the transformative power of this beautiful word, awakening—of realizing our true potential and embracing the boundless opportunities awaiting us.

In this book, I've classified chapters and manifestation techniques according to disciplines. Some days you'd want to jog your memory on meridians, and some days you'd want to read up on the subconscious. There will be times when you'd want to look back at the mechanics of the subconscious, and there will be times when you'd want reassurance on why your positive affirmations are important. I promise that every time you read it, I'll be with you on that very step. Supporting you, cheering for you, and rooting for your manifestations to materialize in the physical realm. What you seek is already yours. I know it.

The power of manifestation lies within each of us, waiting to be awakened. It's a force that can transform our lives in profound ways, allowing us to create the reality we desire and deserve. As we embrace the journey of manifestation, let's remember that the power to manifest our dreams lies within us, always and forever.

We've come so far. We've learned to set clear intentions, to visualize our goals with clarity and conviction, and to cultivate a positive mindset that propels us forward. We've discovered the importance of gratitude and the transformative power of self-love. In the end, it's not just about what we manifest, but who we become in the process. It's about embracing our true selves, stepping into our power, and living our lives with purpose and passion. As we close this book, let's carry with us the knowledge that we can create our own destiny with the help of God, and that anything is possible when we believe in the power of manifestation.

So, with love, gratitude, and immense faith that your lives will be better off from this point on, I'd like to stop writing and go back to my own wonderful life. I promise to say a little prayer for you, my dear reader, irrespective of time, and send off positive energies your way.

May you have a wonderful life. May you wake up.

With love and light,

Razan Abdelkarim Al Fahoum

References

Chapter 2

Craiker, K. (2022). As above, so below: Meaning & usage. *Pro Writing Aid Blog*. https://prowritingaid.com/as-above-so-below-meaning

Einstein, A. (1905). On the electrodynamics of moving bodies. *Annalen der Physik*, 17(10), pp. 891–921.

Maxwell, J. (1865, 31 December). A dynamical theory of the electromagnetic field. *Philosophical Transactions*, 155, pp. 459–512.

Mohrhoff, U. (2016, April). The quantum mechanics of being and its manifestation. *Cosmology*, 24, pp. 1–8.

Chapter 3

Alive Water (2023). *Water experiment by Dr. Masaru Emoto*. https://www.alivewater.ca/dr-masaru-emoto/

Abella, J. et al. (eds). (2024). Wave-particle duality. In *Encyclopedia Britannica*. https://www.britannica.com/science/wave-particle-duality

Calamassi, D. & Pomponi. G. (2019). Music tuned to 440 Hz versus 432 Hz and the health effects: A double-blind cross-over pilot study. *Explore*, 15 (4), pp. 283–90. https://doi.org/10.1016/j.explore.2019.04.001

Cheney, M. (2001). Tesla: Man out of time. Touchstone.

Cleveland Clinic (2023). *Breathwork for beginners: What to know and how to get started.* https://health.clevelandclinic.org/breathwork

Dean, J. (2020, March 8). *Brainwaves and manifestation – The 5 types of brainwaves.* Life's Breakthroughs. https://lifes-breakthroughs.com/brainwaves-and-manifestation-the-5-types-of-brainwaves

Emoto, M. (2005). *The hidden messages in water.* Atria Books.

Feynman, R. (1964). Field energy and field momentum. *The Feynman lectures on physics.* https://www.feynmanlectures.caltech.edu/II_27.html

Hunt, V. (1996). *Infinite mind: Science of the human vibrations of consciousness.* Malibu Publishing.

Siegel, E. (2023, August 24). *The entire quantum universe exists inside a single atom.* Big Think. https://bigthink.com/starts-with-a-bang/entire-quantum-universe-inside-singleatom/#:~:text=At%20both%20a%20classical%20and%20quantum%20level%2C%20an,and%20subatomic%20interaction%20we%E2%80%99ve%20ever%20observed%20and%20measured

Tavel, M. (1999, October 21). What exactly is the 'spin' of sub-atomic particles such as electrons and protons? Does it have any physical significance, analogous to the spin of a planet? *Scientific American.* https://www.scientificamerican.com/article/what-exactly-is-the-spin

Chapter 4

Longhurst, J. (2010). Defining meridians: A modern basis of understanding. *Journal of Acupuncture and Meridian Studies* 3(2), pp. 67–74.

Nucleus AI (2024). Japanese wisdom on the three faces everyone has: Art of persona. *YourStory*. https://yourstory.com/2024/01/japan-three-faces-concept-explained

Chapter 6

Cascio, C. et al. (2016, April). Self-affirmation activates brain systems associated with self-related processing and reward and is reinforced by future orientation. *Social Cognitive and Affective Neuroscience*, 11(4), pp. 621–9.

Cherry, K. (2024, January 31). Emotional intelligence: How we perceive, evaluate, express, and control emotions. *Very Well Mind*. https://www.verywellmind.com/what-is-emotional-intelligence-2795423

Mayo Clinic (2024). *Hypnosis*. https://www.mayoclinic.org/tests-procedures/hypnosis/about/pac-20394405

Medical News Today (2019). *A guide to EFT tapping*. https://www.medicalnewstoday.com/articles/326434

Seysener, L. (2011, September 22). Time Line Therapy®: An advanced technique from the science of neuro linguistic programming. *Australian Journal of Clinical Hypnotherapy and Hypnosis*, 32, pp. 40–48.

Tu, Y., Zhang, L., & Kong, J. (2022). Placebo and nocebo effects: From observation to harnessing and clinical application. *Translational Psychiatry*, 12, article 524. https://www.nature.com/articles/s41398-022-02293-2#citeas

Author Bio

Razan Abdelkarim Al Fahoum was born in Kuwait, and with her Jordanian heritage, American education, and a residency in the UAE spanning almost two decades, she has acquired a unique and diverse perspective on life. Al Fahoum is the visionary CEO and Founder of Elegant Qubes Decorations, a company she single-handedly started from scratch a few years ago, and one that has gone on to become a leader in exhibitions, technology, architecture, and interior design in the UAE.

Embarking on her entrepreneurial voyage at the tender age of twenty-four, Al Fahoum possesses a rich tapestry of experience in multiple realms: event management, interior fit-out, exhibition design, emotional well-being, mental health, motivational guidance, and youth career and life coaching. Her unwavering dedication to excellence has been duly recognized through a plethora of accolades from the UAE's government and several other respectable organizations.

Al Fahoum holds a degree in International Business from Halifax Community College (USA), specializing in Economic Strategy & Marketing. Alongside her academic qualifications, she is an emotional intelligence coach with a master's degree in Neuro-Linguistic Programming. Al Fahoum is also a Neuro-Cognitive Development specialist, a clinical linguistic hypnotherapist, and has a certification in Feng Shui. Her earnest-ness to continue learning has also led her to dabble in aircraft engineering. Al Fahoum's brilliance garners national attention, and she features prominently in esteemed media outlets in the UAE, where she generously imparts her wisdom on business and investments, technology, design, exhibitions, event manage-ment, and fashion.

Al Fahoum is adept at guiding and supporting people through life's nuanced transitions. Whether navigating the leap from one career to another, transitioning from school to college, or embarking on new personal journeys, she empowers people to embrace change and overcome obstacles. Her approach melds modernity with tradition, reflecting in everything she does—her life choices, designs, personal style, and leadership style. She firmly believes in designing a life that mirrors self-awareness, high morals, ambition, and giving back to the community

When she is not working, Al Fahoum loves spending quality time with her family and making everlasting memories to cher-ish later. She enjoys horse riding and ice skating when she wants to unwind. Her love of reading and writing has always been a part of her self-expression, which led her to write her first book, "Wake Up Now."

Al Fahoum is dedicated to inspiring young entrepreneurs, women, and anyone aspiring to uncover their life's purpose and propel personal growth. She helps people transform their lives, leading them to be in harmony with their aspirations. With her credentials, Al Fahoum offers tools and techniques delving into the workings of the mind, fostering a positive outlook and steering the self toward abundance, fulfillment, and manifesta-tion. She guides people towards their true calling, and her posi-tive perspective has been instrumental in changing the lives of many. With her book, "Wake Up Now," she hopes to reach many more.

Currently, Al Fahoum resides in Dubai, surrounded by loving family, friends, and protégés, all of whom seek her guidance in manifesting their best lives.

Notes

www.ingramcontent.com/pod-product-compliance
Lightning Source LLC
Chambersburg PA
CBHW030529210326
41597CB00013B/1075